FOOTBALL
how much do you really know?

Also available
in this series:

EXPLORING WOODS
Peter Schofield

Have fun with
ORIGAMI
Robert Harbin

Have fun with
SEWING
Janet Barber

IS THERE LIFE IN OUTER SPACE?
Peter Fairley

PONIES AND YOU
Sue Turner

S.O.S. WILDLIFE
true Survival stories
Victor Edwards

THE WILD WEST
Robin May

FOOTBALL
how much do you really know?
JOHN TAGHOLM

Illustrated by
Robin Anderson

Independent Television Books Limited, London

INDEPENDENT TELEVISION BOOKS LTD.
247 Tottenham Court Road
London W1P 0AU

© 1975 John Tagholm

ISBN 0 900 72742 X

Printed in Great Britain by
Staples Printers Ltd.
of Kettering and London

To Thomas

This book shall not, by way of trade or otherwise, be lent, re-sold, hired out or otherwise circulated without the publisher's prior consent in any form of binding or cover other than that in which it is published and without a similar condition including this condition being imposed on the subsequent purchaser. The book is published at a net price and is supplied subject to the Publishers Association Standard Conditions of Sale registered under the Restrictive Trade Practices Act, 1956.

Distributed by WHS Distributors

CONTENTS

Introduction
1 The rich and the poor: Arsenal and Darlington Football Clubs 8
2 The Pitch 13
3 Footballs 17
4 Football shoes (and boots) 24
5 Shirts, shorts, socks and shinpads 30
6 Referees and linesmen 73
7 The groundsman 51
8 The goals 60
9 Floodlights 65
10 Scouts 72
11 The players 82
12 Keeping them on their feet 92
13 Safety 98
14 Football and television 102
15 Football: past, present and future 108
16 Your club dossier 121
Words 125
Books on football 126
Acknowledgements 126
Index 127

INTRODUCTION

This is not an ordinary book about the most popular sport in the world. It's a book that will tell you more about what footballers *wear* than the goals they score; it will tell you how a football club is *run*, not what position it finished in the League. It will tell you about the work of *football scouts* and about the brilliance of the players they discover.

Football was a marvellous book to write. I had to talk to all sorts of people with very different jobs in football — from making footballs to looking after football pitches. In my travels up and down the country I watched football shoes being made and examined new designs for players' kit. I talked to the men behind football — the managers, the manufacturers, the groundsmen; and to the people who constantly have the spotlight on them — the players. I learnt a lot of surprising facts about soccer.

I visited Arsenal, one of the richest clubs in the country, and Darlington, a much poorer club run on a much smaller scale. I talked to players who play local weekend soccer in the local park. I found out about referees' whistles and trainers' bags.

And, of course, I went to lots of football matches. After a while strange things began to happen at these games. The more I learnt about football, the more fascinating the game became. When the players ran out I immediately looked to see what sort of football shoes they were wearing and what sort of strip they had on (long-sleeve/short-sleeve/nylon/cotton). Before the kick-off I looked at the pitch to see the work the groundsman had been doing; I checked the type of nets the club used and counted the number of policemen and St John's Ambulance men on duty. When the trainer ran on to attend an injury I tried to see what he brought out of his 'magic bag'. Sometimes I watched the referee instead of the players: what kit he was wearing; what signals he was making to his linesmen. I knew the type of football the teams were playing with and what the goalposts were made of. Instead of just watching a football *match* I was watching a whole world of football.

Perhaps you play for a team, one of the hundred thousand or more teams in Britain. Or perhaps you just like to watch. Either way, I hope *Football* can add to your enjoyment of this magnificent sport. Writing it certainly made the sport even more exciting for me.

Football: the most popular game in the world. Here Jim Cumbes, Aston Villa's keeper, brilliantly saves a penalty from Oxford United's Derek Clarke.

1
THE RICH AND THE POOR:
Arsenal and Darlington Football Clubs

There are ninety-two clubs in the Football League. Just a handful are rich; the rest get by one way or the other, finishing the season with a small profit or, more likely, a loan from the bank.

Arsenal is one of the rich clubs. Visiting Highbury Stadium is like being shown round a smart hotel — marble floors and walls and long corridors with lots of doors leading to splendid facilities. You can tell what sort of club Arsenal is just by looking at the red and white minibus which is used to take players and staff from the stadium to the training ground some distance away; the number plate of the bus is AFC 2. And inside the main hall, hanging over the big window marked 'Enquiries', is the name plate from an old steam train named after the Arsenal. That's the sort of club Arsenal is, the kind of little extra you would expect from a world-famous football club that won the 'double' — the League Championship and FA Cup — in 1971 and has won the League Championship no less than eight times.

Darlington Football Club has never been in the First Division. In fact the highest position it has ever achieved in the League is fifteenth in the Second Division — and that was in 1926. Arsenal play in Highbury *Stadium*, with a tremendous capacity for 63,000 spectators; Darlington's Feethams *Ground* will take 20,000 at a pinch and is surrounded by trees and next door to a cricket pitch.

So what does it really mean, playing at opposite ends of the Football League? Above everything else it means that Arsenal can have a regular average gate of around 30,000 people, while Darlington has to get by on gates of around 1500 spectators. This is the key factor which affects everything else the clubs do.

Running a Football Club

The best way of showing the differences between the two clubs is to look at how much money each spends. Arsenal, with a massive stadium and big crowds, needs to spend around £25,000 a year on just hiring policemen and gatemen for their games. This is approximately twenty-five times as much as Darlington, who are very much aware that just six policemen can cost the club as much as a valuable £70.

Arsenal has a full-time staff of 100, while Darlington employs only 24 people — and remember, 15 of these are players. The total wage bill for Arsenal comes to something like £400,000 a year, while Darlington pays out around £30,000 to its staff. It is at least 130 times more expensive to look after the upkeep of Arsenal Football Club than Darlington, a difference amounting to something like £100,000 a year.

Both Arsenal and Darlington have advertising hoardings round the pitch and on the stands; these bring the First Division club thousands of pounds a season, Darlington a few hundred.

Darlington Football Club is proud that through careful planning and good management it finishes each season with a small profit, which is more than can be said for many much bigger clubs. To achieve this profit, Darlington usually has to sell at least one player a season, probably for a sum that doesn't even run into five figures. Buying and selling players at Arsenal usually involves hundreds of thousands of pounds and is very rarely done just to help the club's finances.

Like Arsenal, Aston Villa has splendid facilities. Here are individual baths for the players and the big bath for the whole team

and the huge changing room for the home team (prepared for a practice session)

Who works for a football club?

Preparing for ninety minutes' worth of football a week is a full-time occupation for many people. The bigger the club the more people are involved. The secretary, the man who arranges fixtures and handles the paperwork, will usually have an assistant and perhaps four office staff. For away games travelling and hotel arrangements have to be made. For home games programmes must be prepared, police and St John's Ambulance men booked, music sorted out for half-time. A big club, running three teams, will have three trainers and a doctor; it will probably have two groundsmen and perhaps a maintenance foreman as well. There will be gatemen, commissionaires, stewards, scouts, laundry staff and the juniors with their coach. While Arsenal have a full-time staff of 100, they employ many more people part-time who come in on match days. When Spurs won the 'double' in 1961, a total of 383 people were employed full- and part-time by the club. Smaller clubs, however, have to operate with the minimum number of people.

Football is not a rich sport. Don't imagine for one minute that £300,000 transfers mean that clubs have plenty of money. Far from it. Clubs have to organise their finances very carefully and are constantly thinking of new ways to raise more money — match sponsorship, for example, where a club sells all its advertising space to one advertiser for a particular game. Most clubs are now looking at ways of paying their bills without having to rely completely on gate receipts.

A few years ago the Arsenal Supporters' Club gave £40,000 towards improving conditions on one of the terraces at Highbury, which was almost as much as Darlington Football Club spent on *everything* that year. But don't think that Darlington Supporters' Club doesn't help out; recently they completely redecorated the changing and refreshment rooms at the club — themselves.

This book will examine more closely everything to do with football. Sometimes you will see that Arsenal and Darlington and the other ninety League clubs do things differently. But they play the same game, with the same rules. For a start, they all play on a *pitch*.

2
THE PITCH

You may never have visited Wembley Stadium, but you're sure to have seen matches played there on television and you've probably heard commentators talk about the 'wide-open spaces of Wembley'. What exactly do they mean?

In fact the commentators are referring to the size of the pitch, 105 metres (115 yards) long and 68·5 metres (75 yards) wide. Well, is the pitch at Wembley any larger than those in the Football League? The answer is no. Many people, commentators included, make the mistake of thinking the pitch *must* be bigger because international matches are played there. In fact Wembley is considerably smaller than some League pitches. For instance, it's 4·5 metres (15 feet) shorter than Doncaster Rovers' and 4·5 metres (15 feet) narrower than Orient's.

Many League clubs have different-sized pitches

What about League pitches? Are they all the same size? No. Leighton James, Burnley's flying winger, is probably a lot happier playing at Manchester City than at West Ham, because at City's ground, Maine Road, he's got 8·2 metres (27 feet) more to play in than at Upton Park, West Ham.

Although all pitches in the Football League *look* the same size, very few are actually the same length and width. Some measurements, of course, have to be the same size — the 6-yard box, the penalty area, the centre circle and the penalty arc (these measurements, as Law 1 of the game explains, are known as *appurtenances*, which must be the most unusual, and unused, word in soccer). But as for length, this can vary from 91·4 metres (100 yards) to 118·8 metres (130 yards), and width from 45·7 metres (50 yards) to 91·4 metres (100 yards).

Of the twenty-two clubs in the First Division as many as seventeen have different-sized pitches. Some vary by only a few metres, but just compare one of the biggest, Maine Road, Manchester City — 106·9 metres (117 yards) long by 72·2 metres (79 yards) wide — with the smallest, Upton Park, West Ham — 100·5 metres (110 yards) long by 64·0 metres (70 yards) wide. A total of 8·2 metres (27 feet) difference for wingers, and just imagine a kick by a goalkeeper which at Upton Park could, with the wind behind it, land in the opposite goal but which at Maine Road would land 6·4 metres (21 feet) in front of the goal. Quite a difference.

In the Second Division, eighteen of the twenty-two pitches are of different sizes. In the 1974-5 season, when Manchester United were in the Second Division, their pitch was the longest at 106 metres (116 yards); the shortest are at Fulham and Oldham (100·5 metres, or 110 yards). Orient, along with Third Division Hereford, has the widest pitch in the Football League — 73·1 metres (80 yards). That's an astonishing 9·1 metres (30 feet) wider than West Ham's pitch.

There are twenty-four teams in Division Three and twenty have different-sized pitches; the longest at Wrexham and Aldershot — 106·9 metres (117 yards) — and the shortest at Halifax and Southport — 100·5 metres (110 yards).

You would think that the super-fit clubs of the First Division would have the biggest pitches, but almost the opposite is true. Division Four has the longest pitch — 109·7 metres (120 yards) at Northampton — and the biggest pitch overall — 107·8 metres (118 yards) by 72·2 metres (79 yards) at Doncaster. Darlington's pitch is 2·7 metres (9 feet) wider than Arsenal's, although they are the same length.

Sport in this country is slowly going metric. The regulations for international matches state that the maximum measurements must be 110 metres by 75 metres (120 yards by 80 yards) and the minimum 100 metres by 64 metres (110 yards by 70 yards). In ten years' time all our pitches will probably be marked in metres. The pitch at Wembley is exactly midway between the maximum and minimum.

Marking a pitch

All lines marked on a pitch, except for the centre spot and penalty spot, must be not more than 13 centimetres (5 inches) wide and must be flat — they may not be marked with a groove or a lump. There is nothing in the regulations to

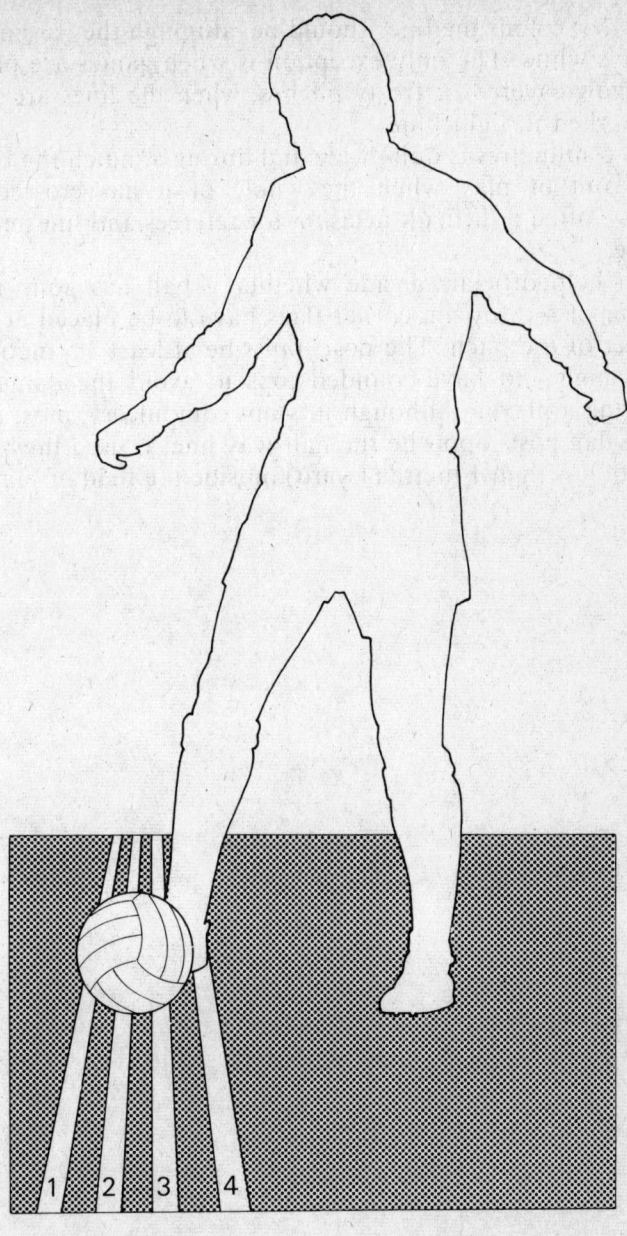

*The ball is only out of play when the **whole** of it has crossed the line, in this illustration it is out of play in relation to line 4*

say what colour the lines should be, although they are nearly always white. The only exception is when games are played on snow-covered or frosty pitches, when the lines are often re-marked in light blue.

13 centimetres is quite wide and during a match the ball is only out of play when the whole of it has crossed the line — often a difficult decision for referees and linesmen to make.

To help officials decide whether a ball has gone for a corner or a throw-in, corner flags have to be placed at each corner of the pitch. The posts must be at least 1·5 metres (5 feet) high and have rounded tops to avoid the danger of injuring a player. Although it is not compulsory, most clubs have flag posts opposite the half-way line; if used they must be not less than 1 metre (1 yard) outside the field of play.

3
FOOTBALLS

The rain is pouring down and the pitch and players are soaked. But what is happening to the ball? A silly question? Well, not so long ago a first-class football which began a match the regulation weight of between 397 and 454 grammes (14 and 16 ounces) often finished weighing considerably more. The ball soaked up the moisture, making it hard to kick and even harder to head. In fact, commentators could be heard saying: 'the players are now finding long, high passes difficult as the rain-soaked ball becomes heavier and heavier.' Today this couldn't happen.

A 32 panel ball speeds towards goal

Footballs: what are they made of?

Modern footballs — the ball you play with at school, the balls you see in Football League matches — all have a special waterproof coating which keeps them the regulation weight throughout a match, no matter how hard the rain falls.

That's just one of the many changes between a ball of twenty years ago and today's football. For instance, if you heard a team was playing with a plastic ball you would probably imagine a lightweight ball, perfectly round without any stitching at all. It might surprise you to learn that many professional games are now played with all-plastic balls — usually called 'synthetic' balls. The 1974 League Cup Final, for example, was played with a Stuart Surridge 'Cobbler' ball. Instead of leather the ball is made of a rubberised canvas called Porvair, which doesn't stretch as much as leather but, when it does, it stretches evenly, keeping the ball perfectly round. The regulations state that the ball must be between 686 and 711 millimetres (twenty-seven and twenty-eight inches) in circumference. The 'Cobbler' has a nylon lining which brings it up to the regulation weight.

The Stuart Surridge ball is used by many First Division clubs and the materials are so reliable that the ball is guaranteed not to go out of shape for twelve months. Synthetic balls bounce, fly and act in exactly the same way as leather balls. In fact one leading manufacturer believes that before long all footballs will be made of synthetic materials.

There is nothing in the Laws to say that a ball should be made of leather: 'Leather, or other approved materials', Law 2 states. A great deal of research goes into testing new materials, which have to be approved by the FA, the Football League and FIFA (the international body controlling football) before they can be used in important matches. Testing is essential; for example, tests showed that synthetic balls have to be stitched together with hemp thread because nylon thread, used in leather balls, would cut into the plastic.

Footballs: how big?

Footballs come in five sizes, one to five, although the first three sizes are rarely used. Schoolboy Internationals are played with a size four ball (these usually have thirteen panels), which is 2·5 centimetres (one inch) smaller than a full sized ball. Whatever these balls are made of, the materials must not be 'dangerous to players'. Old leather balls used to have lace-up bladders and occasionally a lace would cut the head of a player; today valve balls are used.

The ball must be pumped up by the home club to 1·5 kilograms per square centimetre (fifteen pounds per square inch) pressure before a game. The referee will check this before kick off, usually by just feeling the ball, and he is the only person who can change a ball during the course of a game. It must be difficult for a referee to know that the ball is exactly the right pressure, unless, of course, he has a special gauge. At the 1966 World Cup Final, Slazenger, who supplied the match ball, had an expert at Wembley with special equipment to make sure the pressure was correct — he also checked the ball at half-time.

Footballs: patterns and colours

Just as synthetic balls are creeping into the game, so are thirty-two panel balls. Most footballs you see today have only

It is virtually impossible to tell the difference between a synthetic ball (plastic) and a leather ball with a waterproof cover. The Astroball (centre) is synthetic; the Brazilia (right) protected leather. These are 18 panel balls. More and more clubs are using 32 panel balls (left). You will never see a patterned ball used in an English League game.

Modern balls do not change weight even in the wettest conditions.

A traditional 18 panel ball made by Zephyr

The more modern 32 panel ball

eighteen panels. Gradually, however, the thirty-two panel ball is taking over because it keeps its shape better. On the continent most professional balls have thirty-two panels, usually multi-coloured — black and white, red and white, red and yellow. You will never see a multi-coloured ball like this used in an English League match — the FA doesn't approve of them. In Scotland, however, they are in regular use.

Most professional balls today are white, although yellow and orange balls are available and are played with in snowy conditions when a white ball would be difficult to see. Sometimes an orange ball is used in floodlit games; a white ball can get 'lost' in the glare of the lights.

Footballs: how many?

For the FA Cup Final the referee has a choice of thirty unmarked balls from which to select the match ball — ten yellow, ten red and ten white. A white ball is nearly always picked. Football League clubs use a variety of manufacturers' balls — Mitre, Gola, Minerva, Adidas, Cobbler. See if you can find out which your team uses.

How many balls does a club use in a season? Arsenal use about seventy balls a season; two are bought for every home match. The balls cost around £13 each, so Arsenal spend more than £500 a year on balls. A new ball works its way down through the club, from the first team to second team, eventually ending up as a practice ball (unless, of course, the match in which it was first used turned out to be special — for example, if a player scored a hat trick and was presented with the ball as a memento). Darlington, which runs only one team, uses about thirty-five balls a season.

The general opinion among clubs and manufacturers is that a ball will last one season only. It takes a tremendous hammering and even the best balls — some can cost as much as £25 — can go out of shape.

Looking after your football

Your football should last you much longer. Perhaps, however, you have a punctured ball that you no longer use. Some manufacturers make a very inexpensive bladder sealer which is pumped into the ball to seal up the hole. This is a very cheap and easy way of saving your football.

Remember, too, to wipe your ball dry after use and to let it down slightly if you're not going to use it for some time — this will prevent it from going out of shape. Never put a football against a radiator or in front of a fire — either would also make it lose its shape.

4
FOOTBALL SHOES (AND BOOTS)

Older football supporters will still claim that the Spurs team of the early sixties, or the Arsenal side of the 1930s, was better than any side playing today. In a sport like athletics, claims like this are very rarely made, because today the modern athlete is quicker, fitter and stronger than his equivalent of thirty years ago.

The same applies to soccer, and apart from actual performances on the field there is no better way of showing the differences than by comparing the equipment worn by footballers in the past with the gear they wear today. No matter what people may say, today's footballer, with lightweight, tailored shirts, shorts and stockings, made of special materials which allow his body to 'breathe', must make him more efficient than the footballer of yesterday, who wore baggy, unstreamlined shirts and shorts, which absorbed sweat and rain and restricted movement.

From boot to shoe

There is no better way of comparing old and new equipment than by looking at the development of what a footballer has worn on his feet. It is the story of the development of the football *boot* into the football *shoe*.

Let's take the two extremes first. In a Manfield shoe catalogue of 1911 four football boots were shown, ranging in price from 10s 6d (52½p) to 14s 6d (72½p). The catalogue mentions that they were used by 'noted men' and 'throughout the football world'. As you can see top right, the boots were big, heavy, rugged and high-sided. They were made entirely of leather — uppers, soles and studs — and were basically the same, despite the difference in price. They had only six studs — four in the front and two in the heel. This type of boot remained the same for approximately fifty years; you could still buy a pair in the late 1950s.

Boots *in a Manfield catalogue, 1911*

Boot/shoe *Manfield Hotspur Continental Mark II, 1955*

*Today's lightweight soccer **shoe** and training shoes showing special grips*

Compare those boots with the lightweight Gola shoe (bottom left page 25). It is made of kangaroo skin, has a lightweight moulded sole, with four studs in the heel and nine in the front. It is shaped to fit the foot perfectly and is as comfortable as a pair of casuals.

In between the old and the new there was a period when players' footwear was neither a boot nor a lightweight shoe. Manfield, who manufactured the big heavy boots already mentioned, were making the Manfield Hotspur Continental Mark II soccer boot in 1955 (middle page 25). The leather was fairly thick and it still had a very solid toe-cap; but it had much lower sides and a moulded, multi-studded sole. Low-sided boots made in those days were always described as 'continental'; the lightweight shoe had been in general use abroad for many years. In fact, Argentinian players were wearing low-cut shoes as early as 1920. But in this country, even in the late 1950s, many professionals preferred to stick with the boot, believing it to be safer and better for kicking. Gradually, however, the football shoe took over.

Certainly, the low-cut shoe does make the foot more vulnerable to injury. Manufacturers, however, emphasise that their shoes are made to fit 'like a second skin', with special support for the foot, and a reinforced heel to protect the vulnerable achilles tendon from injury. Some shoes have special long tongues to protect the top of the foot from injury, although the long tongue tends to come in and out of fashion.

Some footballers have now started wearing a high-sided 'shoe' to protect their ankles — still lightweight, with a soft toe, but with special built-up sides.

As long as *all* players wear shoes then the chances of injury are reduced; just the size and weight of the old boots made them dangerous. The old leather boot tended to soak up moisture and become heavier as the match went on.

Adidas (named after the head of the firm Adi Dassler) have a sports museum in Germany with a display of more than 250 pairs of football boots and shoes. The boots made between 1900 and 1914 weigh over 550 grammes (about twenty ounces) each; as late as the 1950s the weight had dropped by about 85 grammes (three ounces). This might not seem very much but it has been estimated that during a match a footballer takes approximately 10,000 steps. The saving of 85 grammes on every step means that 2032 kilos (two tons) less weight is lifted by the player during ninety minutes. The saving now is even greater; Adidas's lightest shoe weighs as little as 212 grammes (eight ounces). Pick up a pack of butter and you'll see just how light that is.

Today's regulations state that a player 'shall not wear anything which is dangerous to another player'. Studs can be plastic, leather, rubber, aluminium or similar material, as long as they don't stick out from the sole more than 19mm (three quarters of an inch), nor be less than 12·7mm (half an inch) in diameter. Aluminium and polyurethane studs are now preferred, especially by referees, because, unlike nylon studs, they cannot by scuffed into sharp edges. No metal plates are allowed in the manufacture of soccer shoes.

Football shoes: different types

The professional footballer today will have three kinds of football shoes: a pair with a nylon sole for screw-in studs for use on soft, muddy pitches, a pair with moulded, multi-studded soles, for use on harder surfaces; and finally a pair of training shoes with no studs at all, for use on bone dry or very icy pitches, and for training on hard floors.

The sole of a training shoe is specially designed to 'grip' hard surfaces. For example, the sole of the Gola training shoe is flat, with cleats and suction holes (as you can see bottom right on page 25). The basic design was the idea of Bill Shankly when he was manager of Liverpool and wanted to equip his side with shoes for extra hard surfaces, especially icy conditions. The grooves catch on the hard surface and the round holes act as suction pads to give extra grip.

Football shoes: how many does a club need?

Arsenal runs three teams; if each player has three pairs of shoes, that makes a total of nearly a hundred pairs of shoes. These are kept in the boot room (not a shoe room), where they are cleaned, repaired and re-studded by apprentices and

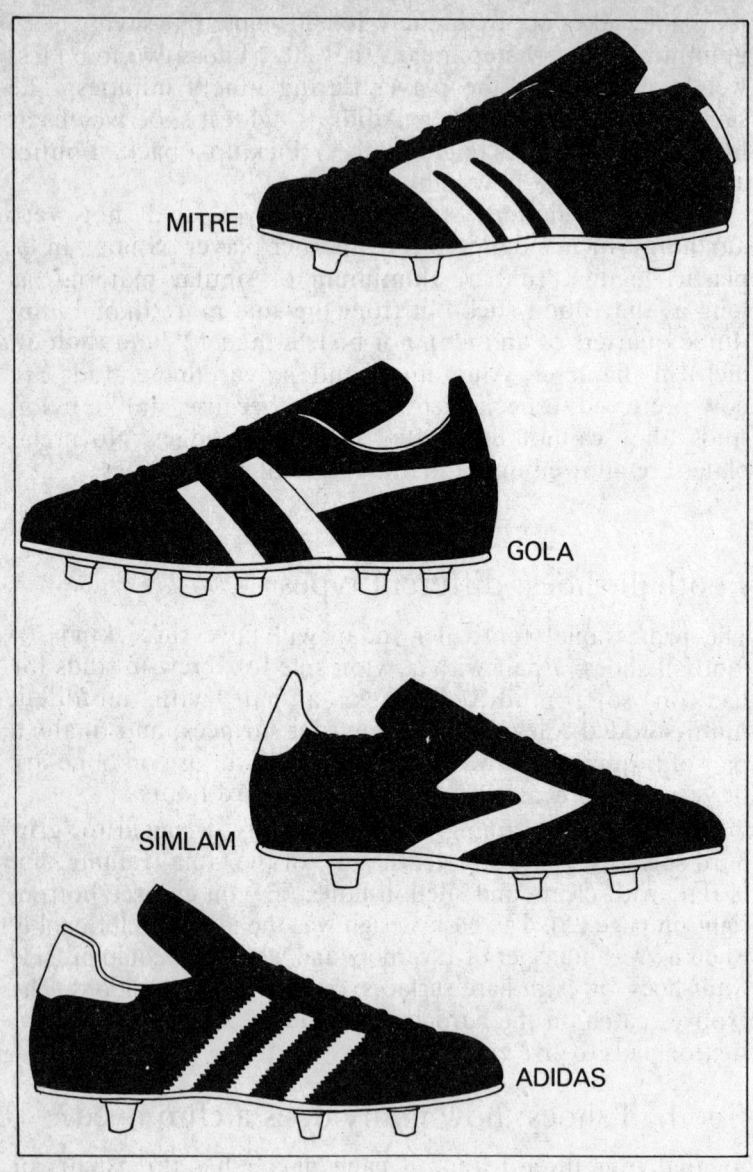

Some teams wear the same make of shoe. Some wear five or six different makes. Which types have you seen?

hung on pegs or stored in lockers. With so many shoes around how does a player recognise which are his? At Arsenal and Darlington the players' initials are hammered into the soles with small brass nails. Other clubs use similar methods. Moulded sole shoes have numbers or initials painted on, or special identification tags sewn on.

Players become very attached to their shoes, especially if they have had a run of successful games with a particular pair. Several football clubs are supplied with shoes by one manufacturer and often the shoes are sent back at the end of the season for 'repairs'. Often the shoes are torn and worn away in places, with the soles coming away from the uppers. It would be easier to issue a new set, but players insist that their favourite shoes be repaired and returned. Players hate 'breaking in' a new pair of shoes because they might blister their feet, so they sometimes get apprentices to do it for them.

Football shoes: how are they made?

The modern football shoe is a highly sophisticated piece of work. Over forty separate operations go into making a football shoe — selecting the leather, clicking (cutting out the various shapes), closing (stitching the pieces together), lasting (a last is a wooden shape which determines the size of the shoe), cementing or riveting the sole to the upper.

Your football shoes

A pair of very good football shoes will cost around £15; they might last a professional a season. The same pair should give you more wear if you look after them. Do *not* use dubbin on your shoes if they are made of leather — it stops the hide from breathing. Use an aerosol wax spray or ordinary boot polish. Let your shoes dry naturally — it is bad for the leather to be put next to something hot when wet.

It is hard to imagine how the modern football shoe can develop further, but that's probably what Mr. J. J. Law thought in 1891 when he invented the screw-in stud!

5
SHIRTS, SHORTS, SOCKS AND SHINPADS

For most of the century soccer strip remained basically the same — long baggy shorts, billowing shirts, heavy woollen socks, and, as we have seen, big, heavy boots. It is only

What they used to wear. Alex James (above) famous Arsenal forward of the 1930s. Huge shorts and thick boots. Stanley Matthews (opposite) famous Blackpool forward of the 1950s. Twenty

recently that players, managers and most of all manufacturers have woken up to the fact that every week footballers stand in front of thousands of people to *entertain*. Other types of entertainer — singers, comics, actors — often with much smaller audiences, have always dressed knowing they were going on 'public view', and that it was good for their 'image', as well as their own confidence, to look good. Now, at last, footballers are following their example.

years between the pictures and yet the shorts are just as long. The boots are slightly lighter – but the socks are thicker.

The new kit

In the last few years the revolution has begun to take place. New, smarter, more comfortable and more exciting soccer gear has appeared, helped by technical developments and particularly by the impact of colour television on football.

Big changes in football, however, come about slowly, because the FA and Football League, as well as many directors and managers, are very wary of change. One director of a leading First Division club, when asked by the team manager for permission to go ahead and buy a smart new redesigned strip for his team, replied: 'You're not turning the game into a circus!' Well, in many ways soccer is like a circus; unless the crowd is entertained they will, in time, lose interest.

But there are important changes taking place. Just look at Leeds United. They have made an important point of not only playing well, but also looking good. Leeds had a new strip — shirts, shorts, socks, tracksuits, right down to tie-ups — designed for them by Admiral, who make many of the brand new designs in soccer and supply several League clubs. When he was Leeds's manager Don Revie, despite being basically superstitious about changing the club's strip, decided it was not only a good idea for the overall look of the team, but also for the players, who, just by turning out in the new style strip, earn a special royalty on the number of Leeds United strips the manufacturer sells.

Many managers are concerned that their players, who really have a very short career at the top, should have every opportunity to make extra money. The system works very well. The players know that if they look smart *and* achieve a good League position more people, i.e. local club sides, will buy their club's strip. The players win, and so does the manufacturer (when Q.P.R. joined the First Division a few seasons ago, sales of their strip shot up, so the system does work).

Leeds United led the way in changing the *image* of football, making it more glamorous and colourful — as it is on the continent. All Leeds' first team squad have tracksuits with their individual names printed on the backs. On the continent

Football strip 1900, 1950 and today. 1950s strip (bottom right) had changed little since 1900–thick, baggy, cotton shirts and shorts; heavy woollen socks and big leather boots with 'solid' toe-caps. Today's strip (centre), normally made of nylon, is lighter and healthier.

many teams play in shirts with the club's name printed on; others have advertisements on their shirts, something which would not be possible in this country at the moment. This form of advertising will come, however, and the money it makes will do a lot to help clubs in the lower divisions who are continually looking for new ways to improve their finances.

It was clubs in the Third and Fourth Divisions who first began experimenting with new style strip. Home colours have to be registered with the Football League, but away strips can be changed without notification. So clubs began to take the opportunity of trying out new ideas with their away strips.

For important games, like FA or League Cup Finals, teams usually have new strips, along with newly designed tracksuits. In 1974, however, when Manchester City reached the League Cup Final, they were refused permission by the Football League to wear a new *styled* strip because the match was not considered to be a true away game.
League to wear a new *style* strip because the match was not considered to be a true away game.

Football shirts: what are they made of?

Until recently, nearly all football shirts were made of cotton. About six years ago, though, cellular, knitted nylon was introduced, and big changes were on the way. The 1970-71 season saw many teams change over to the new nylon shirts. Nylon has many advantages: it doesn't shrink, it retains its shape, it is stronger and lasts longer, it doesn't run and it gives brighter colours. Cellular nylon also helps the body to 'breathe'. A few clubs, however, still prefer the old cotton strip; both Arsenal and Darlington, for example, still play in it.

At local club level it is estimated that a set of nylon shirts will last a team about three seasons, while cotton shirts would probably need replacing after just one season. Arsenal get through eight sets of their cotton shirts every season, Darlington six. Of course, the shirts take a terrific pounding during the League season and it is important for the strip to be in good condition for every match. A complete set of shirts for Arsenal costs around £65, so Arsenal spend over £400 every season on shirts alone.

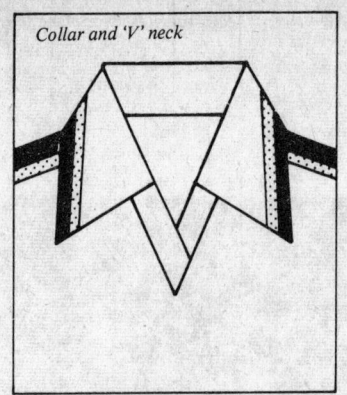
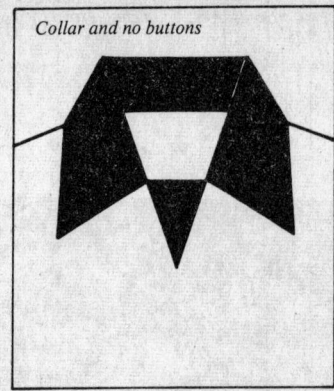
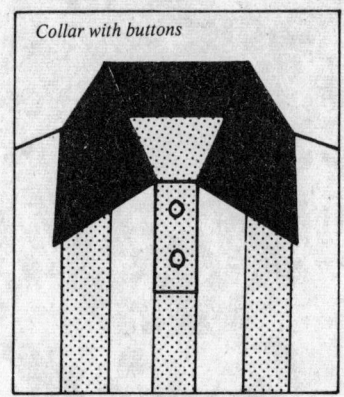
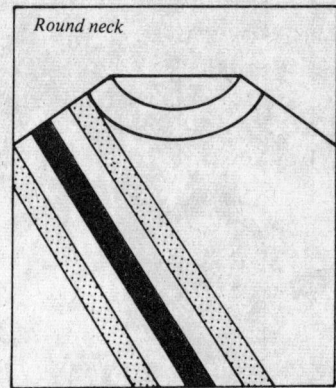

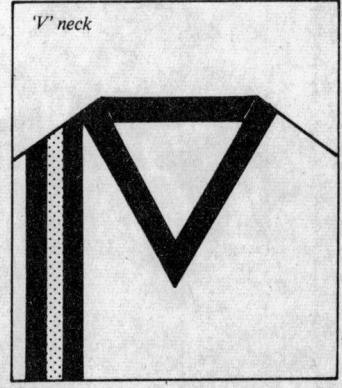

How many different styles of soccer shirt have you seen?

Arsenal v Leeds. Arsenal in cotton strip Leeds in nylon. Arsenal get through twice as many shirts as Leeds.

England v West Germany 1975. Colin Bell scores, but note the Continental number 2 on Bertie Vogts' shirt. Will British clubs soon be wearing this style of number?

Leeds United's kit is made of nylon, and they need only two sets of home strip and two away sets each season. If Leeds had to pay for a complete kit for the first team — including tracksuits — it would cost approximately £260.

All Leeds players are measured up for their own kit, although this in not done in all clubs — Arsenal, for example, take standard sizes. Big players, like Peter Osgood and Martin Chivers, have shirts made with specially long sleeves.

It is difficult to keep pace with the number of different styles of soccer shirt now being worn by League clubs — 'V' neck, round neck, collar and no buttons, collar with buttons, lace-up. How many different styles (page 35) have you seen?

It isn't the shirts that players worry about most — comfortable shorts are top priority. Admiral make five different waist sizes for the Leeds squad. The new 'V' 'speed' vent in the legs of the shorts is there to accomodate big thighs and to prevent rubbing and ripping. This is a style copied from athletic shorts which have always had a split in the side so that the leg movements while running would not be restricted.

Nearly all shorts and socks worn by League clubs today are made of nylon. One new development, to replace the elastic-topped shorts, are shorts with tie cords, similar to swimming trunks. Leicester City was one of the first clubs to use this type of short. This style, however, has its disadvantages; often, especially in wet conditions, the tie cord is hard to undo after a game and players, exhausted after a match, simply cut the cord in order to get the shorts off.

No matter how much a manager wants his team to appear uniformly smart for a match, some of his players will have particular preferences — a short-sleeved shirt rather than a long-sleeved one, for example. Managers accept this; a player who feels uncomfortable will probably play badly, no matter how much of a professional he is. Many teams change into a clean strip at half-time; coming out for the second half in sweaty, damp strip is rather like starting a match with strip in that condition.

Numbers

In England, the Football Association stipulates that numbers must be worn on shirts, and that they must be at least 23 centimetres (nine inches) high. Most teams have bigger numbers; in fact, the minimum-sized numbers, especially on hooped or striped shirts, are often difficult to make out from a distance. Some teams wear numbers on their shorts as well, and Leeds United now have numbered tie-ups for their socks.

In Scotland numbers don't have to be worn, and some teams just wear them on their shorts.

What do goalkeepers wear?

In League football goalkeepers' jerseys can be one of four colours only — scarlet, royal blue, royal green, or white. The most popular colour is green. Very rarely will you see a keeper wearing a white jersey, the colour being impractical for such a mucky game. In recent seasons, however, Peter Shilton, Stoke and England goalkeeper, has started to wear a very smart polo-necked white top. Shilton is a big man, and the white top, together with white shorts, makes him a very conspicuous figure in a goalmouth, so much so that television commentators have remarked that opposing forwards are distracted and often shoot straight at him. Of course, the opposite could apply; forwards see Shilton quickly and easily and shoot round him. Goalkeepers have to wear colours which distinguish them from the other players and the referee.

Yellow is the one other colour that goalkeepers can wear, but only at international level and only if they play for England. So very few get the chance.

As in the case of football shoes, shirts, shorts and stockings must not be made with materials that might be harmful to another player. Buttons, for instance, when used in the collar type of shirt, have to be protected by an overlapping layer of material. When Peter Shilton had a jersey designed which had buttons and a very fine zip it was rejected by the Football League as liable to cause injury.

One thing is certain: no matter how many changes have recently been introduced into footballers' kit, there are many new things to come. Soon, perhaps, footballers will have their names on their shirts as well as tracksuits; or the team's name.

Peter Shilton, Stoke City and England keeper, wearing the unusual white pole-neck jersey.

With so much strip to wash, most League clubs have their own laundry facilities, with laundry ladies on the staff to cope with the mammoth job.

Shin-pads

Many footballers should be thankful to Mr Sam Widdowson, a Nottingham Forest player, who in 1874 invented the shin-pad. Mind you, they wouldn't be too pleased if they had to wear the kind of shin-pad he designed. They were more like cricket pads, worn outside the stockings and held in place by straps underneath the knee and round the ankle. By the turn of the century shin-pads were being worn inside stockings, but they were still thick and cumbersome, made of canvas or leather, with cane strengtheners. Eventually nylon took over, although for a long time cane remained the basic strengthener. It was found, however, that cane could splinter and cause injury, and today's shin-pads bear very little resemblance to those of only a few years ago.

Some shin-pads, for instance, are made of high density, lightweight plastic called polyethylene. The pads are carefully moulded to the curve of the shin and have foam backing for extra comfort. This backing can be peeled off, washed and stuck back again. The front of the pad has tiny nobbles of plastic at the top and bottom which grip onto the stockings and keep the pad in place. Most footballers, however, strap the pads in place with strips of fine sticky tape around their stockings.

Many clubs are now insisting that their players wear shin-pads in order to minimise the risk of injury.

Footballers, at all levels, can now be seen with special holdalls for their kit, marked with the manufacturer's name — Puma, Gola, Adidas. These bags are waterproof inside and out, and many have special compartments at the bottom for muddy, wet football shoes.

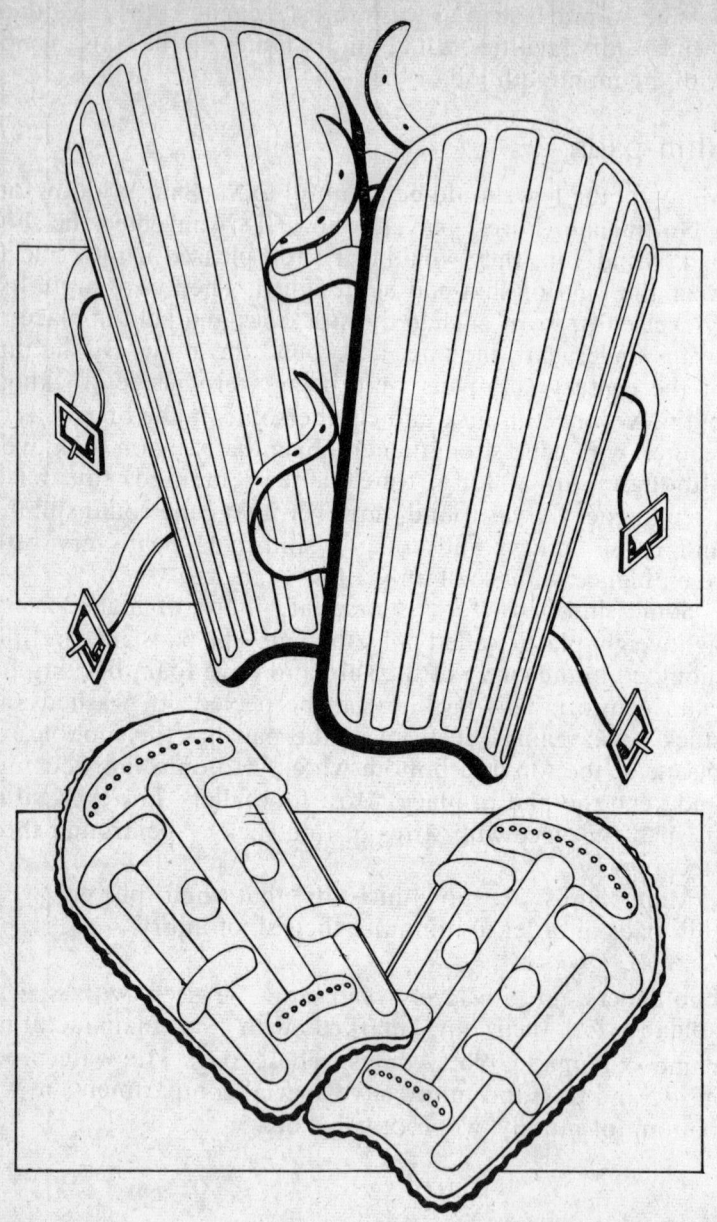

Shinpads, 1874 style (above). More like cricket pads—and nearly as big. Modern shinpads (below) are made of lightweight plastic. The little nobbles top and bottom grip on to stockings and keep the pad in place.

42

6
REFEREES AND LINESMEN

Becoming a first-class referee is very hard work indeed, harder than most people realise. Few referees ever get on to the League list; fewer still ever referee the Cup Final, an achievement regarded by all referees as the highest honour in their profession. In fact, it is probably true to say that it is much easier to become a professional footballer than it is to become a top class referee.

Despite the difficulties of their job, referees are not professionals; they all have other jobs, where they must be able to get time off to become 'part-time' referees. Referees can travel something like 30,000 miles a season, which takes a great deal of time. And all for £17.50 a match.

The referee has to make important decisions quickly in front of thousands of people.

How to become a league referee

For a start, there are only eighty-five referees on the Football League list, twenty-three supplementary referees and 281 linesmen (a Football League linesman is one step away from being a Football League referee). For the fortunate few who do manage to get on the League list, the road will have been long and hard, probably lasting more than ten years.

During those ten years a referee will have slowly climbed through the various stages of promotion. He will have started on a junior amateur league as a Class 3 referee after first passing an examination. It would probably have taken him about two years to get his Class 2 certificate. If he is good — very good — he could, three years later at the very quickest, be graded Class 1 by his local County Football Association. This grade has to be accepted by *all* counties. The referee's name is then placed on a special FA list at their headquarters at Lancaster Gate, London. Even at this stage he will not be called on to referee a big game; he might be a linesman for an early round of an FA Cup tie, but that's as close as he will get to the big time. He can then be recommended to a senior semi-professional league if his marks, obtained while refereeing the best amateur leagues, are high for at least two or three seasons. The semi-professional leagues usually have assessors to mark the referee and if, once again, he scores high marks for about three seasons he will then, at last, be recommended to the Football League. During his time with the semi-professional league he will have occasionally run the line in a Football League game in order to gain crowd experience and to learn from top referees. Eventually, after at least ten years very hard work, he will go on the League list as a referee.

Referees' decisions can be vitally important; an incorrect decision could cost a club thousands of pounds, ruin a player's career or cause hooliganism in the crowd. So it's important that a referee should have a great deal of experience at all levels before taking on a Football League game.

No matter how long a referee has spent in Classes 2 and 3, he will never become a Class 1 referee if he wears glasses; FA regulations allow him to wear contact lenses, but not glasses.

So you have to be dedicated to become a Football League referee. Dedicated, and not very interested in the money the job pays. A referee receives only £17.50, plus expenses, for a League match and cup tie. For international matches he is paid only his expenses. If the match is abroad he gets £10 a day 'out of pocket' expenses as well, which is paid by the home country.

The Cup Final, a nerve-racking experience for the referee and linesmen, certainly doesn't bring these officials nearly as much financial reward as it does the players. The Cup Final referee is paid £25, plus expenses, and he also gets a precious gold medal. In the old days the Cup Final referee was offered the money *or* the gold medal. He always took the medal, something he could treasure for ever.

Linesmen get half the fee of referees, plus expenses. The League Cup Final referee is paid £25 for the game; linesmen receive £12.50 each.

Assessors

A referee controlling a match is watched not only by thousands of critical fans but also by Football League assessors. The assessor system was introduced in 1970; there are eighty-two assessors in all, who closely examine a referee's game and give him marks. The scores for each referee are added up and special bonuses are paid twice a season (after December and at the end of the season) — £100 for referees in the top quarter of the League 'Merit List'; £50 for those in the second quarter; £25 for those in the third quarter and nothing for those at the bottom. Hardly the sort of bonuses that players receive for a good League position, but at least it's something extra to add to a referee's meagre pay.

There is one step higher that a referee can go — on to the FIFA list for international matches. Usually only six referees at any one time manage to reach this stage.

Although it takes so long to get to the very top of the referee's ladder, all Football League referees have to retire at the age of 47. This annoys many of them, who feel that they are experienced and fit enough to go on well into their fifties.

It also means that the time a referee spends at the top is really quite short — perhaps ten or twelve years — say from the age of 35 to 47. On the continent referees continue to have control of top games until they are much older.

Controlling the game

Few supporters ever watch the referee and linesmen during a game. In fact, the more a referee *is* watched, the more this indicates that he is having a poor game and is attracting too much attention to himself. But it is worth while watching a referee at work.

Referees have to work very hard; physically they have to keep up with the game (top referees train regularly and are very fit), and mentally they have to anticipate the game in order to be in the right place at the right time. Nearly all referees follow a set pattern of covering the field — diagonally, from corner to corner, rather than vertically. This enables them to see more of the game and to work in conjunction with their linesmen.

What does a referee have to carry to control a game? He must have a watch (most referees carry two), a pencil or biro, a note-book, a coin and a whistle. Not all referees carry the traditional 'book'; some just have a sheet of card in a plastic folder.

For international matches where language may be a problem, referees carry a yellow card to indicate that a player has been 'booked' and a red card to show he has been sent off.

Not just any old whistle is chosen; today there is a wide range of plastic and metal whistles that vary in sound from deep to shrill. Referees decide which to use for a particular game — depending on the size of the pitch, the closeness and height of the stands, how many people are expected and the general acoustics of the ground.

*Each linesman controls one half of the pitch.
To make best use of his linesmen the referee will
'cover' the sides of the pitch without linesmen—
by running diagonally between the two sides.*

What they wear

There are no universal regulations about what referees should wear, although their equipment is usually black (sometimes navy blue), with a white collar and cuffs. No English team plays in navy blue or black, but since the Scottish side plays in very dark blue, referees in charge of their matches have to wear alternative colours — sometimes maroon or green.

It would be possible, if acceptable to the Football League, for referees to appear in completely redesigned strip. Roger Kirkpatrick, a well known referee, had a special strip made to his own specifications. Made of special cellular nylon, like

Roger Kirkpatrick wearing his special strip.

many of the players' shirts, it has two white stripes on either side of the shirt so that, when he makes a signal with his arms it stands out clearly against a dark background. The pocket in his shirt has a Velcro flap (no button, but a special clinging material which can be ripped open and pushed shut without any fumbling), and there is a back pocket in the shorts. In recent seasons linesmen have appeared with black and white checked shirts so that their signals can be seen more clearly by the referee. Once again, the continental referees and linesmen are way ahead in the design of their equipment — smart, practical and comfortable, but slowly and surely the traditional 'baggy' old-fashioned style of referee's strip is disappearing from our soccer pitches.

Linesmen

There are two linesmen for a game; each controls one half of the pitch. They look for the same things as a referee but are usually better positioned to make decisions on off-side, throw-ins and corners. Linesmen usually carry a spare watch and whistle; their flags are luminescent orange or red. Occasionally during a game a referee will ask a linesman to change his flag because it clashes with a similar colour in the crowd.

In recent seasons an attempt to bring the referee and his linesmen closer together in the control of a game has taken place. Now, for instance, the linesmen will join the referee in the middle of the pitch when the two captains meet for the toss, so they feel more part of the game.

Referees and linesmen usually bring two pairs of football boots to a game, one for wet conditions, the other for dry. The referee will usually arrive about two hours before a game. Some referees are very critical of the treatment they receive from clubs; very occasionally a referee will drive to the ground to find that no parking place has been reserved for him. Some have to change with their linesmen in cramped conditions with only one shower or a single bath between them. A referee cannot take sides, so they are usually rather anonymous people on match days. But a referee can make or mar a game and deserves the same treatment as a star player.

Could you be a referee?

If, after reading this chapter, you still feel like becoming a referee, then there is a simple path to follow. As soon as you are 16, contact your local County Football Association who will put you in touch with your nearest Referee Coaching Officer. At evening classes, once a week for about five weeks, he will teach you the basic arts of refereeing. There is an examination at the end and if you pass you pay a registration fee and your name is entered on the County FA Register of Referees as a Class 3 referee. You are then on the bottom rung of the very long ladder which could, if you persevere, carry you right through to Football League level. There are approximately 18,000 referees in the country; because of the lack of opportunities at the top many drop out very quickly. So, since soccer at all levels is booming, more referees are wanted.

Norman Burtenshaw, a highly respected referee who retired a few years ago, has written an excellent book on his career as a top class referee. It is called *Whose Side Are You On, Ref?** and it will tell you just what it feels like to stand in front of 50,000 people and make difficult decisions.

*Published by Arthur Barker Ltd.

7
THE GROUNDSMAN

'Not many of the thousands who come to watch,' the Arsenal groundsman explained, pointing to the Highbury turf, in excellent condition despite a hard season, 'realise that the lads don't play on North London soil. This is an *unnatural* pitch, a made-up pitch. Like most of the big grounds in London, the soil was brought up from somewhere else.' In fact, Arsenal plays on Sussex soil, brought to North London back in the early 1950s.

The groundsman is taken very much for granted by the football supporter, who will probably only notice his achievements on the opening day of the season, when the green pitch looks like the top of a billiard table. But the groundsman is a vital part of any football club; the bigger clubs, with at least one match a week on their home ground, trust the groundsman to look after their next most important asset after the players.

The groundsman: what he does and when

The day after a match, when the supporters are back at home discussing the result, the groundsman begins to repair the damage caused by fifty studded feet tearing up his hard work. He will have to work quickly — there may be only forty-eight hours to the next game. He will usually begin by replacing the divots, lumps of grass and soil torn out whole. He will then go over the pitch with a brush or drag mat (a heavy chain mail structure, like an open weave metal mat) to open the grass and let the air get through. During the game the grass gets flattened and would suffocate and stop growing unless it was opened out. That's one reason why groundsmen dislike worms; the worm moulds, round blobs of very fine mud which get flattened by players, form a skin over the surface — again stopping the grass from breathing. The brush or drag mat will knock off the moulds and break them up.

Aston Villa's groundsman surrounded by just some of his equipment—mowers, cultivators, hoses, spades, rollers, ladders and more.

At the beginning and end of a season, when the grass is growing, the groundsman will cut and roll the pitch the day before a match, and probably twice more during the week. At Arsenal the grass is kept at just over 2·5 centimetres (one inch) long during the season, but is allowed to grow to about 5 centimetres (2 inches) in the summer to help it thicken. In winter a pitch is usually rolled just before a game, to flatten the surface. Before most matches the groundsman will reline the pitch with a special line-marking machine.

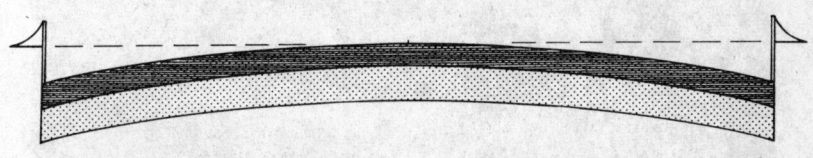

The centre spot of a pitch is also the 'crown'. The pitch should gradually slope away from the centre in all directions to help drainage.

The advertising boards seem to narrow showing the effect of the crown.

The big mower not only cuts the grass but also rolls the surface flat.

As the season goes on and the pitch becomes worn, a skin will often form on top after a wet spell. This acts like a waterproof covering and stops water draining into the pitch, leaving puddles and wet patches on the surface. When this happens the groundsman will spike and slit the surface to get rid of the excess moisture. Rain, or rather too much rain, is the groundsman's biggest problem, and that's why the best soccer pitches have a *crown*. The crown is, in fact, the centre spot and theoretically the pitch should slope away from the crown in all directions to the edges in order to make drainage easier. The difference in height between the centre spot and the touchline at Arsenal is 17·5 centimetres (7 inches); the pitch is rather like a very shallow upturned saucer. Arsenal's pitch is sand-injected at intervals of 30·5 centimetres (1 foot) to a depth of 25·4 centimetres (10 inches); this also helps water drain away. Drainage is also helped by the layers of clinker just below the pitch through which the water passes into pipes which carry it to the ditch which surrounds the pitch.

Les Bateman, Oxford United's groundsman, with a line-marking machine.

During a very dry spell the groundsman has to water the pitch. At Arsenal this is done by sprinklers and a dry pitch there can soak up something like 113,650 litres of water a day. At Manchester City the pitch is criss-crossed with water pipes, set a few centimetres under the surface, so that watering is a simple process and the pitch can be flooded in approximately half an hour.

Although it is an FA ruling that pitches must not be watered forty-eight hours before a game, this is taken with a pinch of salt by most groundsmen. A bone dry pitch is a danger to players, who could easily break an arm in a heavy fall.

More than anything else groundsmen dread a sudden downpour just before the start of a match, not heavy enough to warrant abandoning the game, but sufficient for the surface to be badly churned up by the players.

Sanding is another important job for the groundsman. Sand is usually put down on frosty pitches to give players extra grip on the hard surface. It is a special sand, fairly thick and sharp; fine sand would clog, damage the playing surface and stick to the players' boots. The only exception is the goalmouth where finer sand is used to protect the goalkeeper from grazing his legs.

Cancel the match

Special steps are taken by clubs when playing conditions are very bad and there is a danger that a match might have to be cancelled. A club's fixtures are now so crowded that there is little spare time to rearrange a game. When there is a chance that a match may be cancelled the Football League asks clubs to act quickly and in advance. The visiting club should be contacted the day before to find out their travelling arrangements, both for team and spectators. The referee should be contacted and asked to arrive at the ground the day before kick-off to inspect the state of the pitch *before* the visiting side and their fans begin their journey. As soon as the game is called off it is up to the Football League to inform the national news agencies who immediately tell the newspapers, radio and television of the cancellation.

When it snows everyone–groundsman, players and manager–picks up a spade to clear the pitch.

Although it is the referee who makes the final decision as to whether the pitch is fit enough for a game, he will always consult the groundsman first. No match means no gate, no money and the complications of rearranging the fixture. So when conditions are bad, which they often are during our season, it is up to the groundsman to make sure the game is played. That is an important job.

When the football stops

The groundsman has very little time to relax during the close season; he must get the heavily worn pitch back into perfect condition for the beginning of the next season. He will 'cultivate', i.e. dig up, the goalmouth and the most heavily worn parts of the pitch (including the areas along the touchline, worn smooth by linesmen) and then re-seed. He will also use fertiliser, perhaps once every three weeks if he works for a rich club—fertiliser costs about £130 a tonne. He will allow the grass to grow and thicken, cutting it two or three times a week.

Looking after a football pitch is expensive. Richer clubs can afford staff, equipment and modern techniques. Darlington's groundsman would love to have Arsenal's underground steam heating, which can be used to blow hot air into the pitch to melt frost or to suck away rain — but all he has to work with is a motor-mower (which is also used as a roller), a pitchfork and one sprinkler. At Darlington the local fire brigade helps out by watering the pitch and the local parks department dig and re-seed the goalmouth in the summer.

Arsenal have two groundsmen; they have a mini-tractor with special attachments for rolling, spiking, slitting and cutting, a dump-truck, a sit-on mower and sophisticated sprinklers.

New techniques

Some clubs, like Arsenal with its underground steam heating, are now trying to fight the weather with modern techniques. A few years ago Leicester City introduced a polythene tent to cover their pitch when the weather got bad. The 'tent' covers an area of 8,360 square metres (90,000 square feet) and is inflated with warm air blown in by four electric fans. The cover, which weighs only 1220 kilogrammes (24 hundredweight), takes two hours to put up and is five metres (fifteen feet) high in the centre — enough space for players to train and for the groundsman to carry out his pre-match preparations.

It is also the groundsman's job to look after the goalposts and nets. More about that in the next chapter.

8
THE GOALS

When England played East Germany at the start of their summer tour in 1974, they hit the post three times and the crossbar once. The result was a 1 - 1 draw, but it would have been at least 3 - 1 in England's favour had the posts been a different shape.

But don't the Laws of the game state clearly the size and shape the goalposts must be? Partly. They say that 'the width and depth of the goalposts and crossbar shall not exceed five inches' (13 cm), and that 'posts can be square, rectangular, round, half-round or elliptical'. The posts and crossbars in East Germany were flat and rectangular, like old fashioned goals; the ball rebounded from them entirely differently from the way it would have done from rounded posts, the type used by most English League clubs. A ball shot across the face of a goal will bounce off a square-faced post by continuing on towards the wing; if it hit a rounded post, it would rebound more directly into play in front of the goal.

So goalposts can vary in size and shape, as long as the distance between the insides of the posts is 7·3 metres (24 feet) and the height to the underneath of the crossbar is 2·4 metres (8 feet). You could have goalposts 10 centimetres (4 inches) wide, instead of 13 centimetres (5 inches)—and that extra width could mean the difference of a goal.

Most goalposts are made from the wood of the Douglas fir, although some are made of circular steel. Goals should be painted white, although there is no law to say so. It is the job of the groundsman to make sure that the goals are in good condition. At Arsenal they are washed down every two or three games and during the summer they are dismantled, checked for chips and cracks, and whitewashed. Arsenal have a spare set of goals at the ground in case something should break during a game. If a break happened at Darlington it would present the club with rather a problem — the goals are cemented into position.

Growing in popularlity are full-sized portable goals. Made of tubular steel, with nets attached, they are particularly

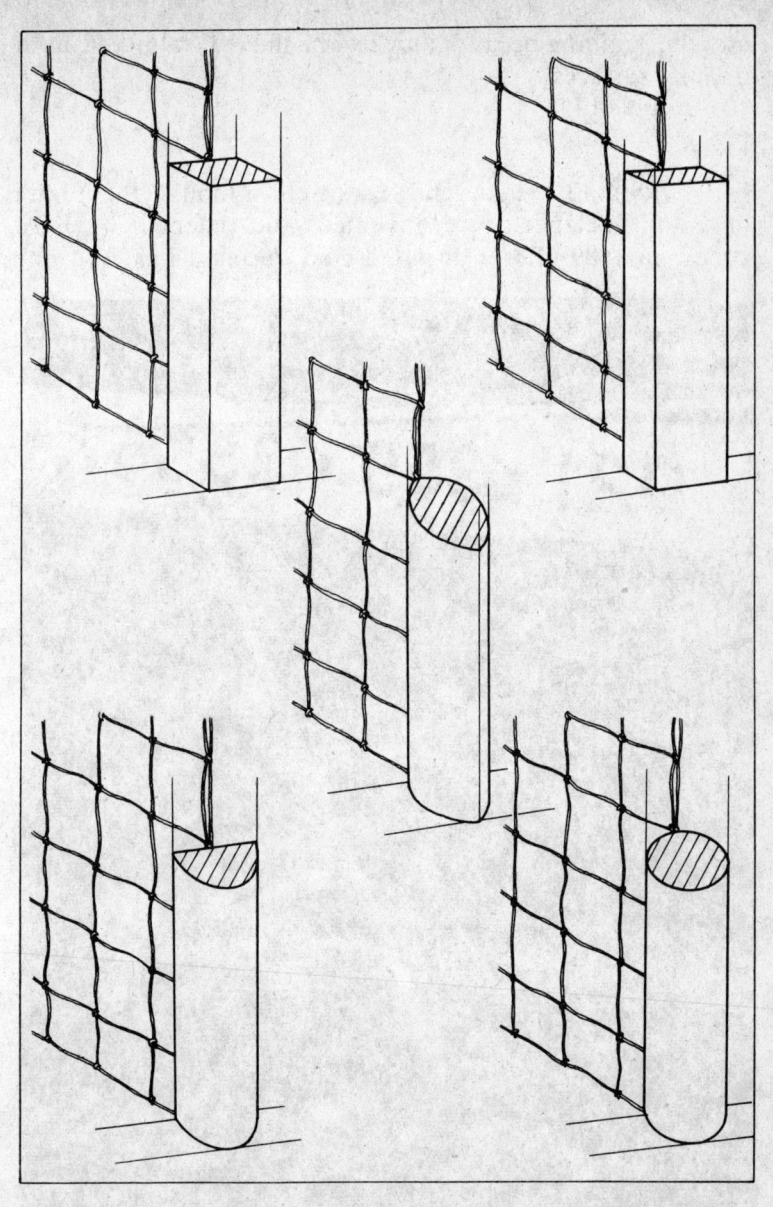

Goalposts can be any of these shapes: square, rectangular, elliptical, semi-round and round.

useful in training because they can be moved on and off hard training surfaces.

Nets

Every Football League club uses nets, although they don't have to. Goal nets were 'invented' and patented by J. A. Brodie in 1889 after a disputed goal during a League game

At Villa Park the nets are the old type, with a wide mesh. At many grounds 'anti-hooligan' nets are used with a fine mesh to protect the goalkeeper from objects thrown from the terraces.

where nets were not used. They were first used in a game at Nottingham Forest's ground in 1891. They were made by Bridport Gundry, who still make nearly all the soccer nets used in Britain today. Things have changed since the first nets were made, however. Today, two types of net are made: the standard 127 millimetre (5 inch) 'knot-to-knot' mesh, and the new 'anti-hooligan' nets. These are specially designed to protect goalkeepers from objects thrown by hooligans in the crowd. Many clubs now use this type of net, including Arsenal, Leeds, Newcastle, Manchester United, Cardiff, Middlesbrough, Huddersfield, Manchester City and West Ham.

You may remember an incident at a match a few years ago, when the ball rebounded from a goal back into play so quickly that there was some dispute as to whether or not the ball had actually gone into the goal. It had, and the incident would not have occurred if the nets had been hung properly; the netting was too tight and the ball shot back into play as though it had bounced off a trampoline. Clubs and groundsmen consult net manufacturers for expert advice on the size and hanging of their nets.

Scoring goals

The ball doesn't hit the back of the net these days nearly as much as it used to. In the 1972-3 season 5034 goals were scored in 2028 games, an average of 2·48 goals per game. In the 1960-1 season 6965 goals were scored in the same number of games. So in eleven years a total of 1931 goals had been lost.

In order to bring goals back into the game the FA and Football League may well have to consider a major revision of the Laws. In 1925 the same problem existed — the number of goals being scored was almost as low as it is today. So in that year the offside law was changed, making a player offside if he had only *two* players in front of him, instead of three. This certainly brought the goals back. In a recent experiment with offside a player could be offside only beyond a line across the 18-yard (16·5-metre) area. This brought more goals and stopped teams bunching in the middle of the pitch. Many managers think that the offside law should be revised to include this new rule. Perhaps the change ought to take place fairly soon — or goalposts, crossbars and nets may soon have to be abandoned!

9
FLOODLIGHTS

Section 4, Paragraph 26, of the Football League Handbook states: 'Any club without just cause failing to fulfil an engagement to play its League fixtures or any of them on the appointed dates shall for each offence be liable to expulsion from the League and/or such other punishment as the Management Committee may determine.' This is one way of saying that all clubs must have floodlights, although nowhere in the regulations are they actually made compulsory. In fact there is only one mention of floodlights: 'A League fixture may be played wholly or in part under floodlight subject to the installation having the approval of the Management Committee.'

There are forty-two matches every season for First and Second Division clubs, and forty-six for Third and Fourth. *Every* club will be involved in more games than these — FA and Football League cup-ties and, for the more successful sides, European games as well. On average each club in the Football League plays fifty-two games a season. That works out at one match a week for the whole year. Since the season always finishes in May, starts again in the middle of August and, according to the rules of the Football Association, no League matches can be played in July, that leaves about forty-two weeks to play fifty-two matches or more.

So in order to get the sort of gates that clubs need to survive, they have to play some games in the evening. In fact the Football League now arranges some fixtures as evening games before the season starts. So all League clubs have to have floodlights.

The history of floodlights

Although the first floodlit game — at Bramall Lane, Sheffield — took place as long ago as 1878, floodlights are really a very recent addition to the football scene. Despite the fact that the first game under artificial light was such a success

All League grounds have floodlights although there is no regulation which makes them compulsory.

(20,000 people came to Bramall Lane to watch and wonder, four times the size of the crowd at that season's Cup Final), the use of lights faded soon after and it was more than seventy years before floodlights began to creep back into the game. Believe it or not, in 1930 the Football Association actually banned clubs from taking part in games played under floodlights. In those days matches had to kick-off at Saturday lunchtime and were only just finishing as the gloom of the early winter evenings came down. This ban lasted until 1951, and even then clubs were allowed to play under floodlights only if they first got permission from the FA or the local County Association.

The year 1951, however, saw the first modern fixture to be played under floodlights — a Football Combination (reserve team) game at the Dell between Southampton and Spurs. But it still took some time before lights were really accepted. In the 1955-6 season replays in the first two rounds of the FA Cup were allowed to be played under artificial lighting. By 1960, though, as European soccer began to become part and parcel of the soccer scene in Britain, the use of lights had become widespread.

Sunderland suggested to the Football League that all postponed League fixtures should be played under floodlights if both clubs agreed, and the first League match under lights took place at Fratton Park between Portsmouth and Newcastle United in 1956. The final acceptance of floodlights came in 1958, when the League agreed that floodlit matches could go ahead without the necessary approval of one or other of the clubs, as long as the lights were of a certain standard.

The introduction of floodlights met with some disapproval from the footballers themselves, who threatened to strike unless they were paid more money for playing evening games. Soon after it was decided that the players should receive between £2 and £3 extra a week for floodlit games.

The tops of two of the floodlight pylons at Villa Park. Note how the actual lamps have been arranged to form the initials AV and how one or two are trained to the terraces.

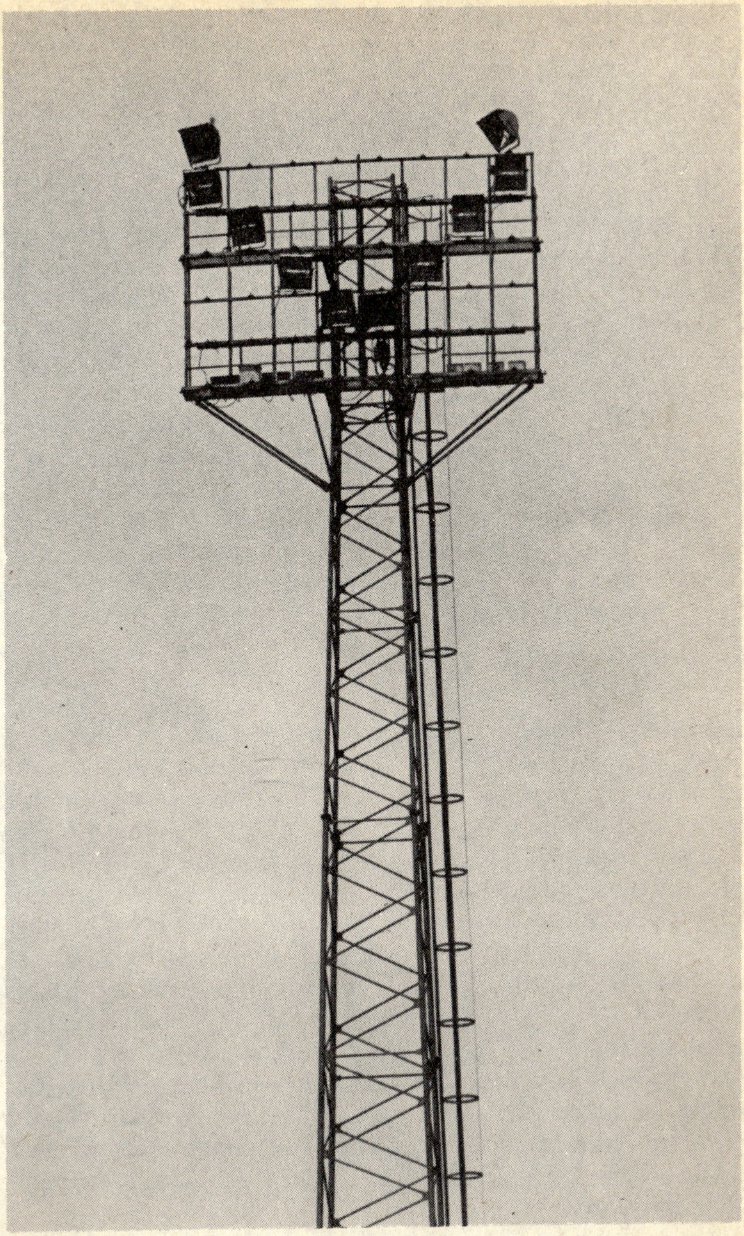

Floodlights: how powerful?

That first match under artificial lighting, way back in 1878, was floodlit by four lamps mounted on poles 9 metres high, one in each corner of the ground. The power came from generators and supplied light equivalent to about 8,000 candles. Today the Football League make sure that floodlights are considerably stronger. The total load required for adequate lighting is put at 90 kilowatts—the equivalent of having about 9000 average-sized lightbulbs hanging above the pitch. This is the minimum requirement. Bigger clubs, with large-capacity grounds of perhaps 40,000 or more, with high stands and terraces, are recommended to use between 200 and 400 kilowatts of power.

The clusters of lights are usually mounted on towers at the corners of the ground, although at Arsenal individual lights are arranged along the top of their two stands, fifty lights on each side. Wembley Stadium has a similar system, although there the lights are arranged in eight clusters, each consisting of twenty-four lights, making 192 separate lights altogether. These new lights, installed a few years ago, cost £25,000.

Installing floodlights

Installing floodlights is expensive and it has to be done very carefully. If you have ever walked into the glare of a spotlight you will know that it can temporarily 'blind' you. To stop this happening to players during floodlit games, the League insists that the average angle from the bottom set of lights to the centre of the pitch must not be less than twenty degrees. Lights that are too low would dazzle. And the lighting must be arranged so that all parts of the pitch are covered and that no shadows — from the stands, for example — are thrown on to the pitch (this sometimes happens during daylight games when the sun is very strong and low in the sky — the shadows on the pitch can make playing quite difficult). When the lights are taken down and cleaned during the close season great care is taken to replace them at exactly the same angles. Some of the lights, of course, are aimed on to the crowd and exits for safety.

An evening game at Arsenal will cost the club about £60 in electricity; the cost of a floodlit game at Darlington would be

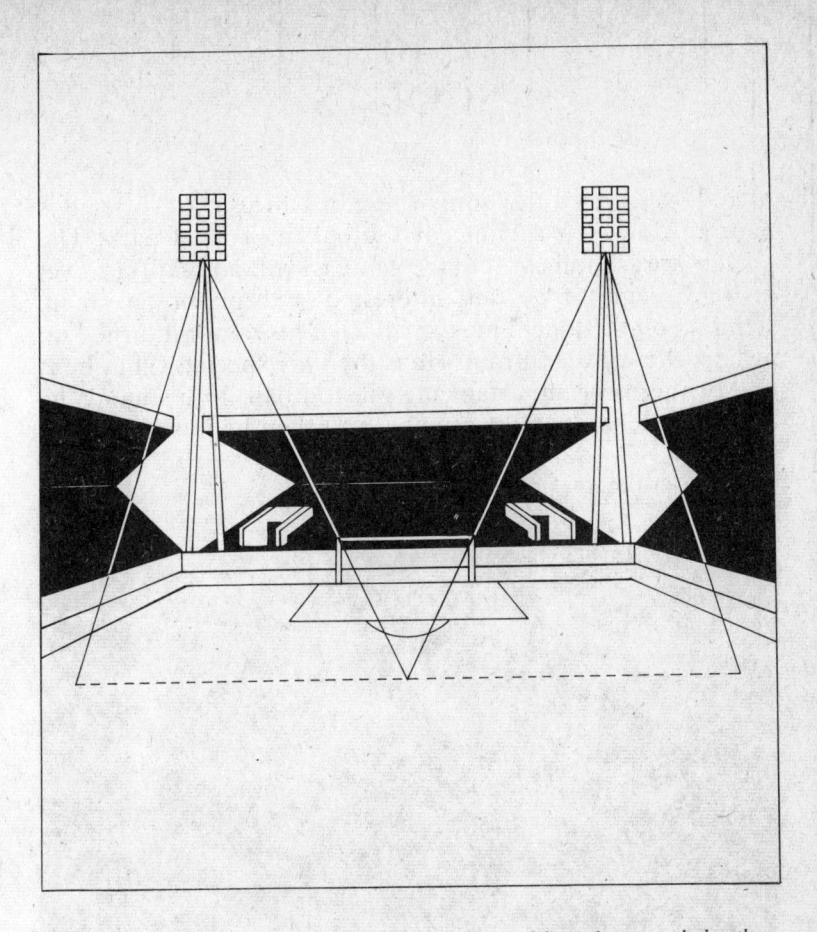

The average angle from the bottom set of floodlights to centre of the pitch must not be less than 20 degrees. Lights that are too low would dazzle.

around £20. It costs more at Arsenal, not only because there are more lights at Highbury, but also because Arsenal's lights are stronger in order to produce enough light for colour television.

In fact, many clubs have had to improve their floodlights so that their games can be televised in colour. Wolverhampton Wanderers, one of the first clubs to regularly use floodlights in the 1950s, was also one of the first clubs to install special mercury iodide lights, which give a special slightly blue light ideal for colour television.

10
SCOUTS

A cold, wet, windy day somewhere in Lancashire. The rain is pouring down on a game of football in a local park. The players are schoolboys, but the game is swift and skilful — yet no one seems to be that interested. Except for one man, standing on the touchline, the collar of his raincoat turned up against the wind and rain. He is the only spectator, but he is one of the most important men in football. In his hands he holds a notebook and every now and then he jots something

Gerry Summers, Oxford United's manager, relies on his scouts to find him young players he can develop into professionals.

down. He stamps his feet hard on the grass, not just to keep warm, but because he is also excited. This lonely figure is a football scout and he is watching one young player in particular — perhaps only fourteen years old — who he thinks might make the grade and become a professional. It's up to the scout to make sure that this young talent is not wasted. He knows the local schools and minor leagues and watches as many games as possible.

Stars of tomorrow? Future professionals often learn their skills playing football in back streets and against walls.

A good football scout could make his club millions of pounds over the years. The scout who was watching that match somewhere in Lancashire thought he had seen a potentially good footballer; he was closely assessing a player who could, in time, be worth more than a million pounds for his club, in gate money and transfer fees. And if the scout made the correct approaches and the boy liked the club, he could get the player for nothing but his wages in the future. That's why scouts are so important. Today League clubs are finding it so difficult and expensive to buy established players from other League clubs that more and more are concentrating on producing their own players, from schoolboy level to Football League status.

What does a scout look for?

Almost every day of the week during the football season that scene in rainy Lancashire is taking place all over the country, as scouts from all the League clubs scan the youngsters in front of them looking for signs that will tell them: 'Here is another Bobby Charlton or Kevin Keegan.' Once a scout spots a player he thinks might make the grade, what does he look for? A good footballer, especially in these days of high pressure soccer, is a combination of many things. First and foremost, though, the scout is looking for skill — ball control, passing, heading ability, shooting power. The next priority is usually pace — how fast is the boy and will his stamina take him through the game? Of course, the scout makes allowances here, for the player's strength and stamina will increase dramatically with proper, intensive training at the club. The scout will then look to the finer points of the boy's game. Is he basically a right or left sided player? Is he determined? Can he control his temper? Has he the character to take the pressures of top class soccer? How well does he run off the ball? Nearly all scouts are ex-players, so they really know what to look for.

How much is a scout paid?

Most scouts are part-time only, and combine this job with other work that gives them a regular income. Scouts are paid travelling and meal expenses, until they come up with a 'find', when they are paid a bonus. A number of clubs do have full-time scouts. Arsenal, for instance, have two, as well as fifteen 'stringers' who keep their eyes open for the chief scouts and are paid for any useful tips they have. Most big clubs like to create a 'network' of scouts over the country in order to see as many young footballers as possible. The part-time scouts and stringers report to the club, or chief scout, once a week.

So what sort of bonuses are scouts paid for coming up with a 'winner'? Here is an average bonus sheet, showing the sort of lump sums that a scout could receive if a player he recommends makes the grade in the first team and beyond into international football.

Schoolboy

For a schoolboy who has been signed as an apprentice professional £50

For an apprentice professional who has been signed as a full professional £75

For this player having made ten full first team appearances — Football League, Football League Cup and FA Cup only £150

For this player having represented his country in an Under-23 International, for first appearance only £100

For this player having represented his country in a full International, for first appearance only £250

£625

Amateur player

For a young amateur player who has been signed as a full professional £75

For this player making ten full first team appearances — Football League, Football League Cup and FA Cup only £150

For this player having represented his country in an Under-23 International, for first appearance only £100

For this player having represented his country in a full International, for first appearance only 250

£575

So a schoolboy who eventually becomes an international could make a scout more than £600. Some clubs pay more than this, many much less. Payment of scouts is, however, going up all the time, as it becomes more and more difficult to find players of first-class potential. But still, scouts could be paid more for the invaluable work they do. As one scout said: 'It's hard work, just like looking for diamonds. There aren't many of them, but when you do find one and manage to dig it out, it's really worth something.'

What happens to a schoolboy player once he has been picked out by a scout?

Usually a good young player is spotted by more than one scout and it is up to the boy to decide which club he prefers (clubs are forbidden by the FA to pay lump sums to parents in order to persuade them to make their son sign for their club). If the boy is over thirteen he registers with the club of his choice as an *associate schoolboy*. This still means that school work and school activities come first, but it does allow the young footballer to receive first-class coaching and to get the feel of a big club atmosphere. Every club is allowed to have up to thirty associate schoolboys on their books. This pool of players is so important for a club — it could provide perhaps half the players for the first team in a few years time.

On leaving school at the age of sixteen the boy can, if his progress has been acceptable to the club (and assuming the boy wants to continue with this club), sign *apprentice* forms. If he is exceptionally good he will stay only a year as an apprentice and sign *professional* forms as soon as he is seventeen, the youngest a player can become a professional. A player cannot continue as an apprentice after his eighteenth birthday, so by then a club will have decided whether or not he can make the grade with them. A club is allowed only fifteen apprentices, although surprisingly many of the big clubs, who can afford to have these extra players, do not keep a full quota of apprentices.

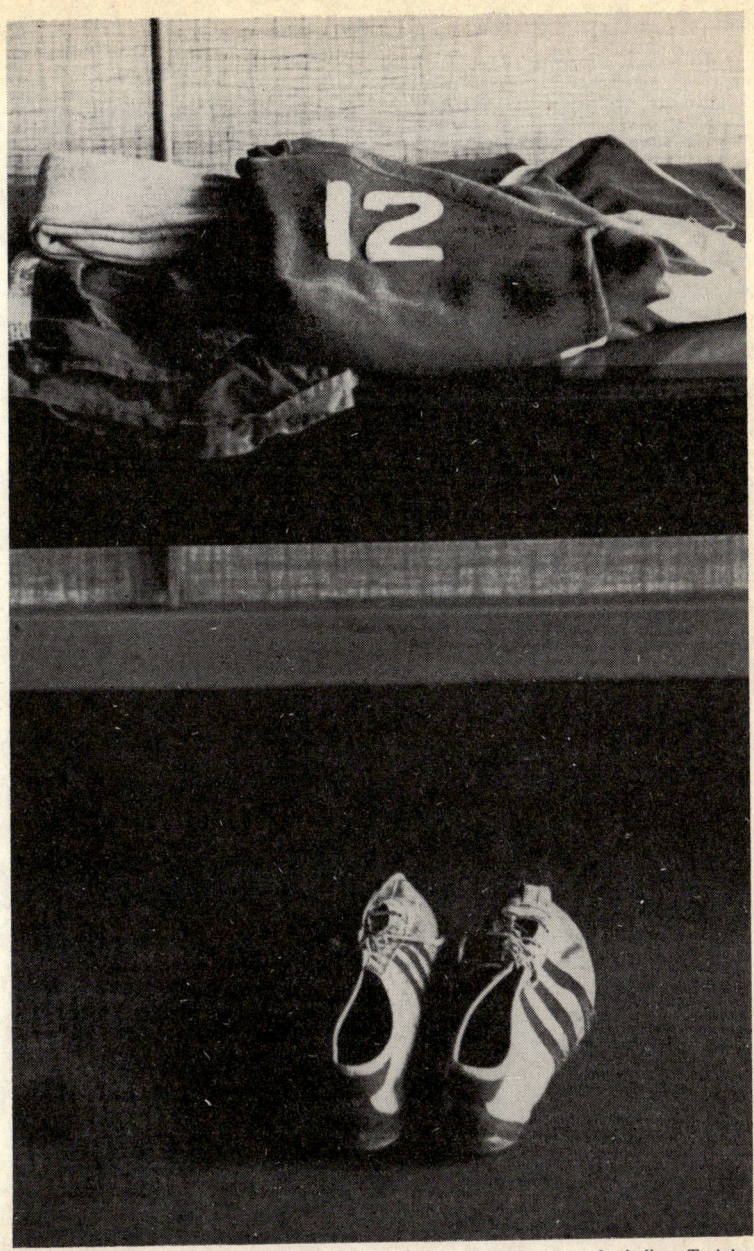

All ready for training. This will become the most familiar sight for young footballers. Training shoes, a heavy, numbered top, old shorts and socks.

Five young boys

The 1974-5 season was one that five young players at Oxford United will never forget. Colin Duncan, Hughie McGrogen, Micky Tait, Les Taylor and Peter Foley all played in the first team for the first time that season. They were all just seventeen years old.

Colin Duncan comes from Wantage, Berkshire, Hughie McGrogen from Glasgow, Micky Tait from Wallsend, Northumberland, Les Taylor from Middlesbrough, Cleveland, and Peter Foley from Bicester, Oxfordshire. They came to Oxford from all over the country. How?

Not only do clubs have paid scouts (Oxford have three) but managers and their assistants have many friends in the game who from time to time tell them of promising young players. And they have men like Fred Ford, Oxford United's Chief Scout and Youth Organiser (the official FA title), one time manager of Bristol City, Bristol Rovers and Swindon.

It was Fred who spotted sixteen-year-old Colin Duncan playing for his school and Wantage reserves and immediately picked him out as a player of great potential.

Micky Tait and Les Taylor, from the same part of the North-East, often used to play against each other at school and were spotted by the same scout when they were fifteen. They were quickly signed as apprentices (the last year that apprentices could sign at fifteen — now they are not allowed to leave school until sixteen).

During the summer Oxford hold 'coaching clinics' where boys from all over the country, picked by scouts and by Fred Ford, meet at Oxford to play one another. This is how Hughie McGrogen was picked by Oxford.

Peter Foley, a local, was easy for Oxford to 'capture'; he was only fourteen-years-old when Oxford first began watching him play for his school side and he joined the club a year later.

All five signed as apprentices with Oxford, played in the Youth and Reserve sides and soon made the grade to Second Division football. Careful, intensive coaching at Oxford quickly pushed these five boys to a high level of football. It is unusual, however, for so many young players to join the first team squad in one season. The boys were inexperienced, but they played well, cost United virtually nothing and are now a vital part of the League side.

The young players of Oxford. Front row left to right, Micky Tait, Colin Duncan, Hughie McGrogen. Middle row left to right, Andy Bodell, Les Taylor, Peter Foley. Back row, Billy Jeffrey. With the exception of Andy Bodell they all played Second Division football when they were seventeen.

What are the wages like?

Between the ages of sixteen and seventeen the Football League stipulates that the minimum wage for apprentices must not be less than £5 and not more than £8, and between seventeen and eighteen, not more than £10. Not much, is it? And apprentices do more than just play football — they clean boots, clean out the changing rooms, help with the equipment, assist the groundsman and much more. In fact, they get to know as much about the club as possible.

But the big rewards are to come, assuming they play for a large club, that is. At Arsenal, the *basic* wage is over £100 a week, but this is no figure to go by, because every season considerable amounts are added in the way of bonuses, bringing the weekly wage in a successful season to around the £200-plus a week mark. The basic wage at Darlington is around £40 a week. Players are paid during the summer; highly paid players take this opportunity to rest, while players in the lower divisions, if they haven't got part-time jobs anyway, work during the summer to add to their basic wage from the club.

Although some people will still complain that top class footballers are paid large amounts of money 'for just kicking a piece of leather around a park', footballers are worth every penny they earn and in many ways should earn a great deal more (see next chapter).

How many young footballers are there?

Some clubs, like Burnley, are noted for their 'youth' policies and seem to have a regular stream of excellent players coming up from schoolboy level to first team status. The more players who are spotted at schoolboy level the better it is for football as a whole. But even the majority of apprentices who are signed on don't seem to make the grade. A survey taken a few years ago showed that only 38 per cent of apprentices actually turned professional. Between 1960 and 1970, of a total of 2126 apprentices signed by League clubs, only 1157 went on to sign professional forms — just over 54 per cent. That leaves a tremendous wastage rate and has many top managers wondering if they are making the best use of the vast numbers of players they have to sift through.

Every season new players need to be tried out in the League, but the system of finding and training young footballers is so haphazard and clumsy. Some managers, like Brian Clough, have suggested that soccer schools should be set up, sponsored by the Football League and FA in conjunction with the government, where promising footballers can be taught to pass exams *and* play football.

Where do young players come from?

There are over 35,000 football clubs affiliated to the Football Association and more than 28,000 school sides in England and Wales. It's from this tremendous pool of players that our future League and International stars are chosen. If you would like to join a local side and want to know how many there are, the best thing to do is to write to the Football Association, 16 Lancaster Gate, London W2 for a list of County FA secretaries and details of teams and leagues in your area. Perhaps, one windy, rainy day, you'll finish a game and be approached by a scout who will suggest that you might like to think about playing for a professional club. You never know.

11
THE PLAYERS

It's hard to realise that as late as 1960 the maximum wage for a professional footballer could not be more than £20 a week (in 1948 it was only £12). In all other soccer playing countries at that time players could negotiate their own contracts and wages, and it wasn't long before our footballers demanded a similar system in this country. Eventually, in 1961, the maximum wage system was abolished and footballers slowly began to be paid the sort of money that their arduous and short-lived careers deserved.

In the last chapter we saw that the drop-out rate of young footballers who decided to try to make soccer their career was very high. Players at the top level don't last for very long either, and yet they provide entertainment for millions of people every year.

A professional footballer's life is vigorous and he has to maintain a strict discipline if he is to remain at the top. Training in all the divisions has now become a highly organised affair and most teams at some stage in the season are probably as fit as they will ever be. Trainers are aware of just how much physical work a player can take — too much exercise can be damaging. The following breakdown of the training routines at Arsenal and Darlington may not seem particularly long and hard, but they are intensive and very tiring. Soccer journalists who have joined in to see what it is like to train with the players have quickly realised just what hard work these sessions are. In the old days training was never like this; often bad weather would mean training was cancelled. Today, big clubs like Arsenal and Everton have superb indoor training areas, almost as big as football pitches. The one at Arsenal, 61 metres by 30·5 metres (200 feet by 100 feet), has a floor of finely crushed red brick for indoor games. Everton's training centre at Bellefield is just as big — and outside there are two full-sized pitches, a training pitch and a shooting box. Liverpool keep one of their training pitches specially muddy so that when the players meet heavy grounds later in the season they have become used to the tiring conditions.

Exhausting work. The author trains with Oxford United. Colin Clarke, United's centre-back, looks on.

A footballer's week

At Arsenal *Monday* is usually a day off, unless the team has played particularly badly on Saturday, in which case they might be called in on Monday to run through the areas where they went wrong and to try to put things right. At Darlington the players go through a hard two-hour session on Monday, basically to build up stamina — exercises, running, circuit training, with very little ball work. *Tuesdays*, *Wednesdays* and *Thursdays* at Arsenal (assuming there is no mid-week game) see two-and-a-half-hour sessions every morning, longer if the trainer feels that it is necessary. At the beginning of the season these sessions tend to be on stamina building; later on in the season, as the players become match fit, there is a greater

Oxford United players go through sprinting and turning exercises around footballs.

85

Villa players go through sprinting and turning exercises around a specific point

concentration on ball work and set moves. *Tuesdays* at Darlington the players go through a two-hour coaching session on ball work — distribution, control, passing, moves. *Wednesdays* they generally have a seven-a-side game amongst the squad to practise running off the ball, passing and general team understanding. On *Thursdays* the team returns to two hours of ball work.

On *Fridays* both clubs have lighter training sessions — about one and a half hours at Arsenal and an hour at Darlington. At these sessions Saturday's match is very much in mind and training is often based around the strengths and weaknesses of the next day's opposition. In this the bigger club, Arsenal, have the advantage, for they employ a full-time 'opposition watcher' who prepares information on other teams to help these coaching sessions. Darlington, run on a much smaller budget, cannot afford to do this, although their manager is well up on the teams in the division.

Saturday is the most important day of the week for footballers. The morning is as relaxed as it can be for the players. For home games Arsenal meet at a golf club on the outskirts of London where they have a pre-match meal, usually a small steak. They meet away from the club to try to ease tension. Afterwards they have a team talk and arrive at Highbury Stadium about an hour before kick-off. At Darlington the players report to the ground about an hour and a quarter before kick-off and then have a team talk from the manager. Both managers will concentrate on particular aspects of each player's game, especially encouraging those players who feel more nervous than the others.

Very few games go by without injury, so some players will find themselves back at Arsenal and Darlington on *Sunday* for special treatment and perhaps a work-out to see how bad the injury is.

Now that's the absolute minimum amount of work for a professional player — about ten hours training a week and a ninety-minute, high-pressure game. But Arsenal, and to some extent Darlington, more weeks than not, will be involved in a mid-week game as well and every other week the team plays away, which often means leaving on Friday and staying the night away from home. The more successful a club is, the more it has to do.

Travelling

Liverpool, for instance, the most consistent League club in European football, have visited thirteen different countries to play their European games — Germany, Hungary, Belgium,

Holland, Italy, Rumania, Iceland, Switzerland, Sweden, Spain, Ireland, Portugal, and Greece. A successful team in Europe may cover more than 25,000 kilometres to compete; and this is on top of the 9500 or so kilometres covered in home competitions.

Travelling is tiring and clubs do as much as they can to make things easy for the players. Coventry City, for example, have a superbly equipped, thirty-seat coach specially designed to make travelling as smooth as possible. It is fitted with reclining seats, radio and stereo, fitted carpets, curtains and blinds. There are special tables with seats around for tactical talks, and a loud speaker system. Food can be prepared on board. Players who are injured in a game can be treated in the coach on the way home on a special therapy couch.

Some players, with highly successful clubs and with international commitments as well, can end up playing something like seventy matches a season — almost two a week. This puts a tremendous pressure on the player and he can become mentally as well as physically tired. It has also led to some injuries developing which are caused by playing too much football. Groin injuries are an example and doctors also warn that such physical exertion can lead to arthritis when a player retires. Most players end up in plaster at some stage in their careers. Removal of cartilages (the fibres that protect the knee joint) is the most common serious injury, and several players have had cartilages removed from both knees. These operations can go wrong and this injury has put paid to the careers of several players.

Players seem to have less and less time to relax during the summer as clubs organise continental tours to keep the team in shape for the next season. And all through the year successful players in all divisions are called on to open shops, speak to schools, take part in ceremonies, promote products and so on. Although these activities mean extra money they also keep the players constantly on the go. Many players, not just the well-known ones, write articles for local papers and magazines and while many of these are actually written by experienced journalists (known as 'ghost' writing) the players

Seventy matches a season–two a week, puts a tremendous pressure on a player.

still have to spend time talking and thinking about themes for their columns.

Footballers and television

Television has made all the difference to a top footballer's life. Now the chances are that instead of 40,000 people watching him at work, the figure might leap dramatically to around twenty million. This means that his every action is closely examined. The stresses of this situation can be so great that some players are now physically sick before a big game. Successful players are interviewed after games and are asked to go on soccer panels which, while giving them film star status, mean extra travelling, extra tension and a programme of events as complicated as any top businessman's (who will probably be paid a lot more). So football is much more than just 'kicking a piece of leather around for ninety minutes'.

An exciting and adventurous manager like Brian Clough, and Derek Dougan, Chairman of the Professional Footballers' Association (PFA), believe that much more attention should be given to the welfare and financial security of footballers. The majority of footballers today lead highly disciplined lives. They have to — so much depends on their being in tip-top condition. Big money is at stake; television is watching. Great players have difficulty in keeping their private lives to themselves. All these pressures have led to a new breed of footballer — well spoken, well dressed, educated and intelligent. Brian Hall and Steve Heighway of Liverpool, for instance, both have university degrees. Many clubs are now insisting that their apprentices do evening classes. All this is done to prepare players for the day when they are too old for top class soccer — probably when they are about thirty-three these days. Some clubs organise business management courses and bring in experts to advise players on how to invest their money and build up business enterprises.

In recent years several players who were household names twenty or so years ago have appeared in the press saying how lost they felt after giving up football. Slowly this situation will disappear as players, knowing they have only ten years or so at the top, prepare themselves early for doing something else after their footballing days are over.

Today a footballer has to be disciplined both on and off the field. In fact a career in football nowadays is much more of a profession than it has ever been before.

12
KEEPING THEM ON THEIR FEET

A leading referee once commented that he could always tell if a player was really injured by the way he fell down. In his experience the player who is pretending to be hurt makes his fall too dramatic. The speed and competitiveness of the modern game, however, has meant that more and more players are going down injured during a game and not all of them are acting. There is more bodily contact in the British and European game than in South American football. So in British football the trainer is seen all too regularly running on to the pitch.

These days an after-match injury list will include items like 'four stitches in gashed ankle' or 'deep cut over right eye and concussion'. Today the big clubs are highly experienced at dealing with every sort of injury. At Arsenal, for instance, the treatment room is just like a hospital with cabinets full of medicines and bandages, medical trolleys (one for emergencies, the other for general treatment) and an 'operating' table surrounded by lamps and equipment. But all this cannot be taken on to the field when a player is injured, so trainers carry a special bag into which they cram what they think is most vital for dealing with the many different types of injury they will have to cope with. The contents of no two trainer's bags are the same; each trainer has his own ideas of what items are most useful.

Really 'trainer' is the wrong word to describe the man who sprints on to the pitch to tend an injured player. Nowadays most club trainers are also qualified physiotherapists, so really it is the 'physiotherapist' who comes on to the pitch. Some television commentators are now beginning to make this distinction. The majority of clubs now have a permanent doctor on their staff; some have two. The poorer clubs in the lower divisions cannot afford to do this, but on match days a doctor will always be standing by. One of the directors at Darlington is also a doctor, which is very convenient.

The speed and competitiveness of the modern game has meant more and more players getting injured.

A physiotherapist treats an injured player. Notice the player on the left using the pain-relieving aerosol on his leg.

What does a trainer carry in his bag?

A surprising amount, as you will see as the Aston Villa's trainer's bag is emptied. A *wet sponge* is perhaps the most important item; icy water on the back of the neck and across the face can quickly revive a dazed player. The sponge now has a rival,

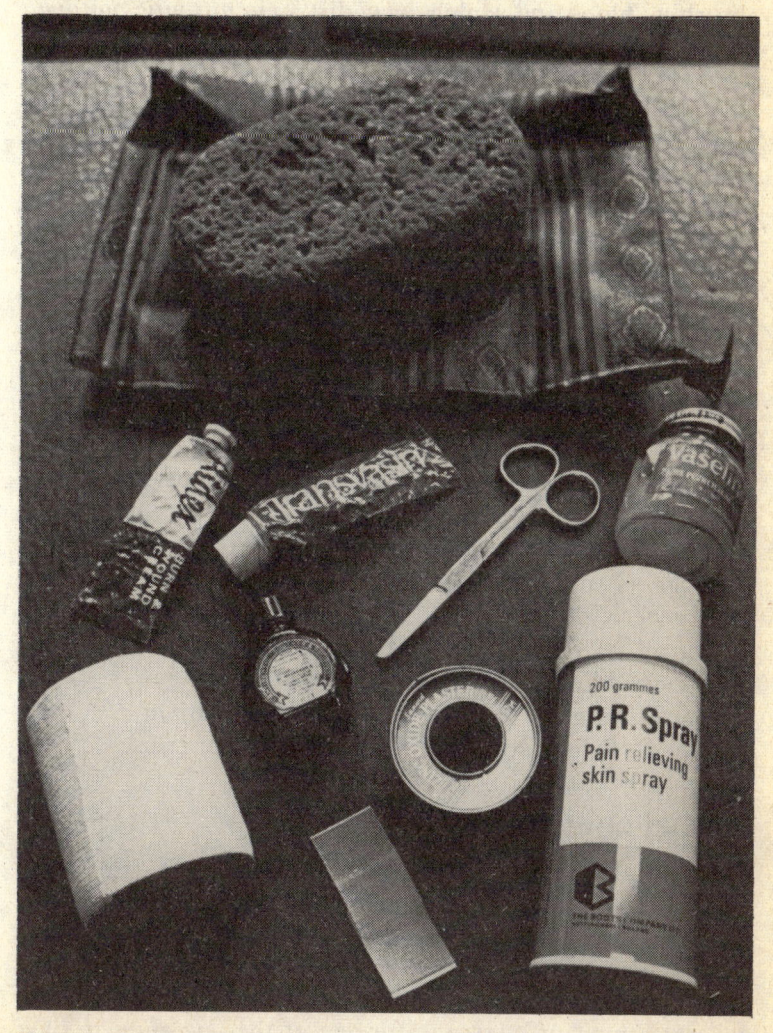

This is what the physiotherapist at Villa brings on to the pitch to tend an injured player: sponge, burn and wound cream, antiseptic, Vaseline, pain-relieving spray, smelling salts, elastoplast, sticky bandage and scissors.

however—*the PR (pain relieving) spray*. This is an aerosol which sprays the bruised part of the body and numbs the area so the player cannot feel the pain. The PR spray has to be used carefully, because some injuries can be made worse if a player continues the game 'unaware' of his injury. *Smelling salts* are carried for bringing round a concussed player; *cotton wool* for absorbing blood and wiping away dirt and *antiseptic ointment* to protect open cuts and grazes. *Elastoplast, lint dressing, sterile pads* and *crepe bandage* are taken out for covering wounds and binding pulled muscles. Before a match players often smear the vulnerable parts of their body— elbows, eyebrows, knees—with Vaseline, so in the event of a collision these areas are partly protected. So the trainer carries out *Vaseline* as well. *Rubber pads* are also carried, to be taped to badly grazed elbows or knees as additional shock-absorbers. If a player strains a leg muscle during a game one of the ways a trainer can stop the injury becoming worse is to put a pad of *sponge rubber* in the heel of the player's boot—this prevents the player stretching his leg as far as he would normally. Unfortunately serious injuries do occur, so the trainer carries a *blow-up splint* and a *triangular bandage* for strapping and supporting broken or fractured limbs. Nearly all players now wear shin-pads and in order to keep them in place stockings have to be kept up with tie-ups. So a trainer carries *strips of bandage* as spare tie-ups. He will also have a spare pair of *goalkeeper's gloves*.

Not all trainers fill their bags like this; some carry more, others less, like Aston Villa's on page 95.

Special trainer's bags are made by various manufacturers. Watch out for the sort of bag your club's trainer uses.

Special equipment

During the week injured players are given intensive treatment in order to get them match fit for the next game. Ultrasonic machines are used for massaging; short-wave diotherm and coil machines for curing muscle strain by deep heat; ultra-violet lamps for curing stiffness and bruising and for general toning up. Arsenal are one of the few clubs to have a sauna bath to help players lose weight.

The treatment room at Villa Park.

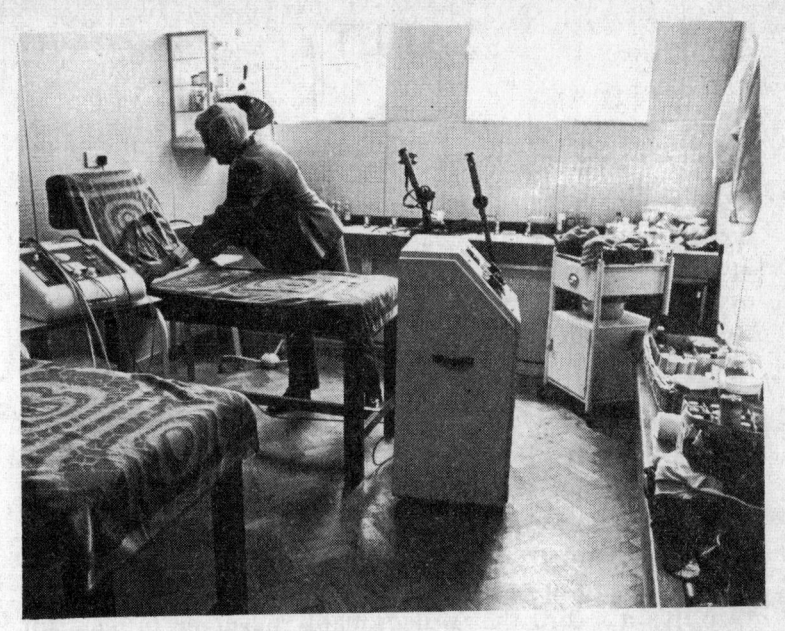

Pulled muscles often occur when a player is cold, which is why teams 'warm up' before a match. Substitutes, who may have to sit out more than half the match before being called out, often have very little time to warm up, so several clubs have now started using special 'sleeping bags' for their subs. The sub climbs into the bag, zips it up and sits on the bench; it keeps his body warm and his muscles loose. When the weather is really cold hot water bottles are sometimes put into the bag as well.

Undoubtedly, professional footballers today are fitter than they have ever been before. With the assistance of modern medical equipment, their ability to recover from serious injury is startling. It is possible, for instance, for a professional to return to the game as little as six weeks after having a cartilage removed, an operation which could keep an ordinary person from playing football for six months. This is not only because the modern footballer is super-fit, but also because club trainers and doctors are becoming more and more skilled at treating soccer injuries.

13
SAFETY

Cramming 60,000 people into a narrow strip of sloping concrete around the edge of a football pitch demands a high degree of organisation and carefully planned safety precautions. Every club fears for the safety of its spectators, dreading the sort of accident that happened in Lima, Peru, over ten years ago, when a disputed goal caused a riot in the crowd during which three hundred people were killed and five hundred injured. Clubs now do all they can to ensure the safety of the spectators and they work closely with the police, local authorities and the St John's Ambulance Brigade.

Soccer crowds are much smaller than they were back in the 1930s. Today police experts examine a ground and estimate the maximum crowd it could hold safely and on match days, when this figure has been achieved, the gates are closed. The all-time record at Arsenal is a crowd of 76,588, achieved in 1946. It's a record that will probably never be broken, for today the crowd limit at Highbury Stadium is 63,000. Manchester United's largest crowd was back in 1920, when just over 70,000 people crammed into Old Trafford to watch a game against Aston Villa; now the ground has a limit of 61,500. The object of limiting the size of the crowd is to create more space for channels in the terraces along which the crowd and officials can move.

Steel crash barriers in the terraces are put there to stop an avalanche of spectators falling on top of one another. As well as crash barriers running *along* the terraces some clubs have now added barriers at *right angles* to the terracing in order to split the crowd into groups and create space between them. Some clubs, like Aston Villa, now use computers to tell them when parts of the ground are full and in danger of overcrowding.

Police
Police are called in for all matches. The police that patrol inside the ground have to be paid for by the club, although

crowd control outside is the responsibility of the police force. The police and club work to the rough rule that there should be one policeman for every thousand spectators (although, of course, it is fairly hard to estimate what the size of the crowd will be beforehand in order to know just how many policemen to order). Very important games, or matches that are felt might cause trouble, have many more policemen, perhaps one for every 250 spectators. In theory, for every ten policemen there should be one sergeant to coordinate their activities. The police watch for troublemakers and are in touch with each other with two-way radios. Before a match they will have been briefed on which section of the crowd to look after and on any specific problems that might crop up.

Policemen patrol ouside the ground as well. This is where the mounted policeman is most effective. Many people — even the toughest soccer hooligans — are frightened of horses and the mounted police are extremely efficient at ordering great crowds of people. Arsenal have found them so useful that the club have a special covered enclosure — a

Safety measure. All clubs have crash barriers to stop large crowds surging down the terraces. Barriers are tested every season.

horse box — at one end of the stadium, big enough to take twelve police horses.

For every match St John's Ambulance men will be on duty to cope with any injuries in the crowd and there is usually a doctor in attendance as well. For an average sized game at Arsenal there will be ten to fourteen St John's Ambulance men; for a crowd of 40,000 there will be perhaps twenty, one man for every 2000 spectators.

Ground safety

The safety aspects of a particular ground are carefully examined by local authorities. They will check that the distance between crash barriers is not more than the statutory 4·7 metres (15½ feet) — at Arsenal they are 3 metres (10 feet) apart; that buildings, tunnels, exits and entrances meet all the safety requirements. During the summer British Inspection Engineers check the strength of the crash barriers; they must be able to withstand a pressure of 1951 kilogrammes per square metre (400 pounds per square foot).

Many grounds are now being altered so that all exits are directly opposite staircases, so that milling crowds at the end of a game can stream straight out of the ground without having to negotiate any dangerous turns. This is one of the areas where many grounds have been found to be particularly unsafe. Unfortunately, nearly every Football League ground was built many years ago and alterations are difficult, expensive and take a long time. Any major changes have to be made during the summer in time for the next season.

Hooliganism

Hooliganism is a threat not only to the safety of spectators, but, in recent seasons, to players as well. In the 1973-4 season hooligans at Newcastle actually stopped a game which, although restarted, had to be played again at a later date. A similar incident at Old Trafford at the end of the season led to the suggestion that deep moats should be dug around the pitches to prevent spectators running on to the playing area. At some grounds, where there is very little space between the pitch and spectators, this would be impossible. An alternative suggestion is that fans should be caged in — that a high wire fence should surround the spectator area. These precautions are in general use in South America and in fact the Manchester United supporters were 'punished' with these fences. Along with Chelsea, they are the only club in the League to have them. It would be sad if the behaviour of a few hundred fans saw the introduction of such measures into all grounds. But if supporters continue to invade pitches the safety of the players will be at risk. So perhaps in a few years time you will have to watch a game with a deep ditch and a high wire fence between you and your team.

Safety measure. The unpleasant side of soccer. The players' tunnel at Villa Park, protected by metal railings and wire mesh.

14
FOOTBALL AND TELEVISION

There are perhaps only five HS 100 *action replay* machines in this country and about two hundred in the world. The action replay machine has probably changed football almost as much as the new offside law did in 1925. If this law brought about a more exciting game with more movement and goals, then the action replay machine has helped the fan at home to look more closely at the skills of the game and enabled football managers and coaches to assess the strengths and weaknesses of their opposition and themselves. The action replay machine has shown not only how precise, fast and athletic football has become, but also how skilful it can be.

Action replay is just one important part of the televising of football. Some people think that televising football matches is destroying the game, reducing crowds and over-exposing the sport so that fans are fast becoming bored with football. Television, however, has brought badly needed money into football, especially into the poorer divisions. In the 1973-4 season, for example, the Football League's television pool, split equally between all the clubs, brought Arsenal and Darlington about £3000 each; that money meant three thousand times more to Darlington than it did to Arsenal. On top of that, advertisers, who know that a club will have games televised, spend money on hoardings around the ground. On average, an advertiser will pay more than £1000 a season for a hoarding in the First Division, about £500 in the Second, £300 in the Third and £100 in the Fourth. A First Division club can make as much as £25,000 a season through this sort of advertising.

But it is not just the money that makes television so important to football. Now more people know about the game than ever before. Today, soccer at amateur club level and in schools has never been so popular — it is becoming increasingly difficult to book a pitch on the local park, so many clubs are playing. Much of this success is due to the televising of football matches. And remember, the more

The HS 100 Action Replay machine. Not much to look at, but, it has revolutionised football. The machine in the foreground allows the operator to turn back the action and then replay it in slow motion.

popular football is at schoolboy level, the more good players will come through to play professionally.

Television has made football international. When England were beaten 6 – 3 by Hungary at Wembley in 1953 (the first time England had *ever* been beaten at home by a foreign side), the nation was shocked. They knew nothing of the Hungarian style of play and assumed that English football was the best and unbeatable. When, in 1972, England were soundly beaten at Wembley by a superb West German side, spectators were sad, but they knew from television that the Germans had been putting together a first class side for some time and that their style of football might well beat England.

Television has made football and footballers more important. Footballers now appear on television to discuss and comment on the game; they are recognised as important entertainers, both on and off the field. This most certainly was not the case twenty years ago. Things really began to change after the first televised football match between Blackpool and Bolton Wanderers in 1960 (the only League match ever to have been shown live).

Televising a football match

The BBC and ITV soccer programmes are organised rather like an actual football squad. During the close season, when the League announces the next season's fixtures, television examines them just like a football club, to get the overall 'shape' of the season. During the summer, when clubs are working out new tactics for the next season, the Big Match and Match of the Day are preparing their teams, designing new sets and methods of presentation.

Which matches can be shown?

Football matches begin with the toss of a coin and so, believe it or not, does the televising of a match. Month by month, ITV and BBC toss a coin to decide who has the first choice of the matches being played. This system does not apply to internationals which are alternated by the two television sides, or the FA Cup Final, the only match in this country which is shown live by both ITV and BBC.

The FA and Football League lay down certain rules which affect which matches are chosen. For instance, every season both the BBC and ITV have to show at least five matches from the Second Division and at least two from the Third and Fourth Divisions. And no FA Cup tie can be televised until the third round. As the season progresses it becomes more and more obvious which games are the important ones and correspondingly the winning of the toss becomes more important.

Once a match has been picked preparations begin. This might be as much as six weeks before the game if it is a ground that the television crew has not visited before. A survey is done to see where cameras should go and whether or not scaffold platforms need to be built for the cameras. A game from a familiar ground is organised very quickly. Cables and the scanner (to beam the pictures back to the studio) are put in place the day before the game, and cameras and sound equipment the morning of the match.

A game will usually be covered by five cameras — four ordinary cameras and one hand-held camera, which is normally positioned behind one of the goals. Three of the big cameras are usually above ground level and one is positioned by the pitch. Production takes place in an EMI mobile control unit; pictures from each camera are fed into this control room and then relayed to the studio where they are recorded, monitored and logged by the research team who make a careful note of the important incidents and how long they lasted. This is a vital job. Their judgement of what is good or controversial will decide what the edited version of the game will be like.

Two editors, each with an assistant, have the job of cutting up the game and putting it back together so that it seems like a whole match. This is where the commentator is so important; he will be careful not to refer too much to incidents earlier in the game which might later be edited out. And he will rarely talk over a goal-kick because this is the best place to edit film. A goalkeeper about to take a kick is watched by one camera; he kicks the ball and another camera takes over. Often, however, the kick you have seen on the first

World of Sport's Brian Moore at work. On his headphones he receives information from the producer. The special microphone picks up the comentator's voice, but not the noise of the crowd. The television monitor tells him which shot the producer is showing. The crib board on his lap contains facts and figures about the two teams.

camera is not the kick you see finishing on the other camera a chunk of film has been taken out.

The commentary is done live and the commentator will have a store of facts and figures about the teams and players to draw on and add to the game as it goes on. Some are supplied by his researchers; many he knows himself and he refreshes his memory a few days before the game. Usually he will have spent a day chatting with the players and his information will be on a 'crib' board in front of him as he commentates.

Televising the big games

Televising a match like the Cup Final is more complicated. As many as seventeen cameras may be used, covering each team, the crowd, the managers, the experts and so on. Pictures are relayed into a control room and the producers have the difficult task of deciding which pictures to show.

It was the 1974 World Cup, however, that showed just how complicated the televising of football can be. It is estimated that in Germany there were 132 commentators and about 2000 technicians from 180 television and radio stations. Pictures were taken by German television and relayed all over the world to be shown live or recorded. The Germans used fifty-six colour cameras, sixteen outside broadcast units and *ten* slow motion action replay machines (at around £45,000 each) in the nine stadiums where the games took place. All this cost £4 million (although, all in all, preparing for the World Cup probably cost the Germans around £50 million). And the footballers in Germany had more people watching them than ever before — almost a thousand million people watched the Final. Some of the pictures coming into the studios in this country had 'bounced off' a satellite 40,000 kilometres away in space.

Without television the majority of people in this country would not have been able to see the best teams in the world play in Germany. They would have been unable to assess the differences in style and temperament of continental teams and compare them with the game in Britain. Television can sometimes be criticised for over-exposing the game. In America, for example, the use of action replay of baseball and American football games was *too* successful. Fans soon became so used to seeing the exciting parts of play immediately slowed down and analysed that they stayed at home to watch and attendances dropped. Not only that, action replay began to undermine the authority of umpires and referees; their decisions could immediately be examined and checked. So now at several stadiums in America huge television screens have been erected so that fans can see not only the live action, but the best bits again, in slow motion. This has brought the crowds back and umpires now make some of their decisions with the help of the action replay machine.

15
FOOTBALL: PAST, PRESENT AND FUTURE

In January 1874 Manchester played a game of football against Liverpool. The following day the *Manchester Guardian* carried this report: 'Yesterday a grand match of football was played between Manchester and Liverpool. The match was numerously attended and great interest was taken by the spectators in the varying fortunes of the game. Before the half-time bell rang, Mr Ribley, one of the Liverpool players, cleverly obtained a goal out of a loose scrimmage. After the play was renewed the Manchester side gained a touch in goal and after a rouge.'

Football is really a very young sport, although we know that a sort of football was played by the Chinese 6000 years ago, by the ancient Greeks and by young apprentices in this country during the Middle Ages. That game between Liverpool and Manchester, which took place only one hundred years ago, shows that even then football still had to get itself sorted out. It was really a cross between rugby and soccer — scrimmages, touch in goal, a rouge (a point, three of which made a goal).

The rules: then and now

The Football Association was formed in 1863 and the famous football laws of that year show what a funny mixture the game was then:

1 The maximum length of the ground shall be 200 yards, the maximum breadth shall be 100 yards; the length and breadth shall be marked off with flags; and the goals shall be defined by two upright posts, eight yards apart, without any tape or bar across them.

2 A toss for goals shall take place, and the game shall be commenced by a place kick from the centre of the ground by the side losing the toss for goals; the other side shall not approach within ten yards of the ball until it is kicked off.

3 After a goal is won, the losing side shall be entitled to kick off, and the two sides shall change goals after each goal is won.

4 A goal shall be won when the ball passes between the goalposts (at whatever height) not being thrown, knocked or carried.

5 When the ball is in touch, the first player who touches it shall throw it from a point on the boundary line where it left the ground in a direction at right angles with the boundary line, and the ball shall not be in play until it has touched the ground.

6 When a player has kicked the ball, any one of the same side who is nearer to the opponent's goal line is out of play and may not touch the ball himself, nor in any way prevent any other player from doing so, until he is in play; but no player is out of play when the ball is kicked off from behind the goal line.

Football 1875. A cross between rugby and football. Caps, long trousers and string for a crossbar.

7 In case the ball goes behind the goal, if a player on the side to whom the goal belongs first touches the ball, one of his side shall be entitled to a free kick from the goal line at the point opposite the place where the ball shall be touched. If a player of the opposite side first touches the ball, one of his side shall be entitled to a free kick at the goal only from a point fifteen yards outside the goal line, opposite the place where the ball is touched, the opposing side standing within their goal line until he has made his kick.

8 If a player makes a fair catch, he shall be entitled to a free kick, providing he claims it by making a mark with his heel at once; and in order to take such a kick he may go back as far as he pleases, and no player on the opposite side shall advance beyond his mark until he has kicked.

9 No player shall run with the ball.

10 Neither tripping nor hacking shall be allowed, and no player shall use his hands to hold or push his adversary.

11 A player shall not be allowed to throw the ball or pass it to another with his hands.

12 No player shall be allowed to take the ball from the ground with his hands under any pretext whatever while it is in play.

13 No player shall be allowed to wear projecting nails, iron plates or gutta percha on the soles or heels of his boots.

Over the next thirty years, up to 1900, football slowly developed from these rules and became the game we recognise today. In 1866 the crossbar was added to the goalposts. Law 7, the one that the *Manchester Guardian* referred to when it reported a 'touch-in goal' was abolished in 1872, when goal-kicks and corners were introduced (although these laws were not necessarily followed by every football club — the touch-in goal in the Manchester-Liverpool game was allowed although two years before that method of scoring had been abolished).

In the 1870s matches were fixed to be ninety minutes long, as they are today, and handball was abolished except for goalkeepers. In 1871 the size of the ball was fixed and those measurements — not less than 27 inches (69 centimetres) nor more than 28 inches (71 centimetres) in circumference — are still the same today. In 1882 the one-handed throw-in was disallowed and the two-handed throw made compulsory. And in 1878 the whistle was introduced for the first time.

In the 1890s football was really catching on and big crowds (for those days, anyway) were turning up. Exactly ten years after the Liverpool-Manchester game 12,000 people watched Preston North End play at Upton Park. But there were still still two big differences between the game then and now — footballers were not allowed to be paid for their efforts, and there was no such thing as a League.

Throughout the 1870s, as the game really began to take shape, some clubs began to pay their players illegally. And then, in 1884, Preston were accused of playing professionals in a cup-tie; they were thrown out of the competition, but complained angrily that there were lots of clubs who paid their players. A year later, in 1885, the FA approved professional football.

So how much were players paid? Just like today, the richer the club the more it could pay and the better the player the more he got. Some players received as little as 10s (50p) a week; the average was probably around £2 a week, although exceptional players with big clubs could be paid £5 a week plus — quite a sum in those days. By 1900 bonuses for success were introduced, contracts between a player and his club signed and, like today, some clubs bought the players their clothes. In 1895 a player was transferred for £250; in 1905 a star moved from Sunderland to Middlesbrough for £1000, a giant sum for that time.

The Football League

The whole business of football was made more competitive with the forming of the Football League in 1888, with one division of twelve clubs — Preston North End, Aston Villa, Wolverhampton Wanderers, Blackburn Rovers, Bolton Wanders, West Bromwich Albion, Accrington, Everton, Burnley, Derby County, Notts County and Stoke. And it was in that order the clubs finished at the end of the first season, with Preston unbeaten after twenty-two games and achieving the 'double' by winning the FA Cup as well.

A Second Division was introduced in the 1892-3 season, but it was not until 1920 that the Third Division, split into North and South, appeared. This system continued until 1958, when the Third and Fourth Divisions were created. Promotion and relegation came in 1898.

So for over seventy years the laws of soccer have been basically the same. Over those years the skills of the players have improved, the organisation of the clubs become more complicated, the amount of money involved in the game much larger, the pressures much greater. And football is now played all over the world.

Can football develop much further?

In Britain a £350,000 transfer deal sets everyone talking: 'Is the player worth it?' 'Can the club afford it?' Most First and Second Division clubs handle hundreds of thousands of pounds a year, nearly all of it made from gate receipts and the sale of players. And yet very few clubs make a good profit — or even a small profit — at the end of the season. Why not?

Walk by a football stadium during a weekday, or in the middle of the summer. The stands are empty, the terraces are quiet. When they are not being used the big grounds are like trans-Atlantic liners going rusty at the quayside. Almost every League ground in the country is under-used; the space they take up is wasted most of the time and they have few extra facilities for the public. On the continent they have a different approach.

In 1973 Johann Cruyff was transferred from Ajax to Barcelona FC in Spain for £900,000. Almost a million pounds for one man. How could the club afford it? Very simply, because Barcelona, like many other clubs in Europe, do not just rely on *football* to make money. Barcelona Stadium is a sports centre and social club which, even before Johann Cruyff arrived, used to make as much as £1000 a day, with more than 50,000 members. The day after Cruyff was transferred the social club took on 14,000 *more* new members and an extra 10,000 season tickets were sold. Barcelona's vast stadium is in use all through the year and every night until midnight.

*Johann Cruyff. Cost Barcelona nearly £1 million from Ajax, but by the **start** of his first season he had made the club that much money in gate receipts.*

'When they are not being used the big grounds are like trans-Atlantic liners going rusty at the quayside.'

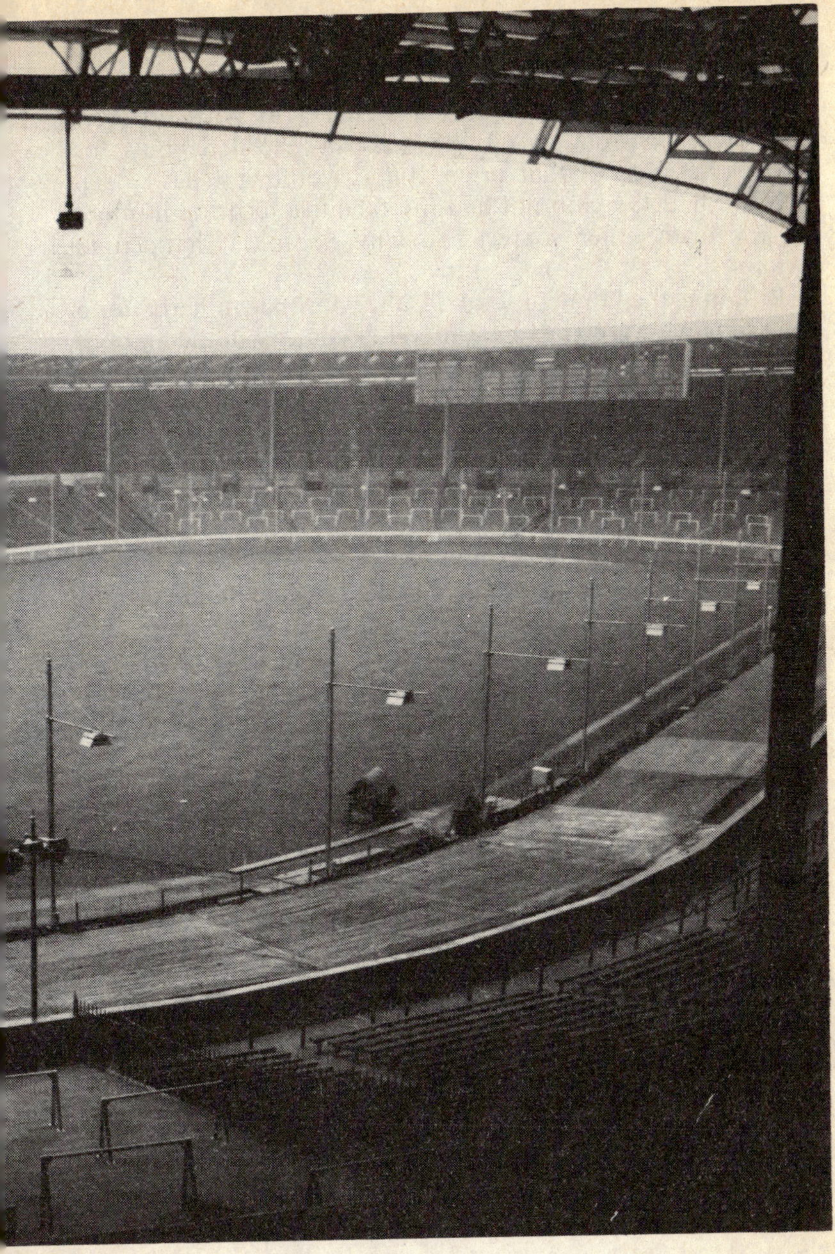

Even before Cruyff had actually kicked a ball in a Spanish league match, Barcelona had got back nearly all the money they paid out for this fabulous player. Before the season started they organised exhibition matches to show off their new star. So Johann Cruyff was an excellent buy for Barcelona, even at that price. But it would not have been possible had the club not had the facilities to bring in more money from other sources. So why doesn't it happen in Britain?

Britain is the home of football; the sport began here. For a long time we were ahead of any other country in the amount of soccer we played, the number of spectators who came to watch and the size and number of our stadiums. As other countries began to catch up, the stadiums they built were more modern and included better facilities and Britain was left behind. Most of our big grounds have had 'face lifts' but major conversions into social or sporting centres would cost a great deal of money. Not only that, during the development, which would take at least a year, valuable gate money would be lost (as Chelsea discovered when they built their new stand). There is only one club in the Football League that has the same sort of facilities as Barcelona, although they are on a much smaller scale. When Bristol City built their new Dolman Stand they incorporated an indoor bowling area and refreshment rooms open to the public. And it makes them money.

In the summer of 1974 Charlton Athletic, with the biggest and most unused ground in the League (capacity 73,000) let out their ground for a pop concert. This brought in some extra money, and put the vast stadium to use. A number of clubs — Everton, Arsenal and Coventry for example — have top quality restaurants open all through the week. Basically, however, most League grounds are wasted. And football cannot afford this.

Barcelona had the facilities, but it was the fabulous Cruyff who increased the membership of the club. Has Britain got the type of star who would make people come just to watch him? George Best, the last footballer who could add thousands of people to every away gate, has now sadly left the soccer scene, with no one to take his place as the most exciting footballer in the country.

The Brazilians began preparing for the 1974 World Cup two years before the event. They spent well over a million pounds making sure that their squad was the best prepared in the world. They even had an expert in Germany checking the quality of hotels, inspecting the changing rooms at the grounds where the team would play, sending back details of German food and so on, so that when the time came the team would have nothing to worry about but football. The Brazilians trained together for three months before they left Rio de Janeiro; the League clubs cooperated by releasing players and lots of money was spent on preparations.

While all footballing nations agree that the four Divisions of our Football League are the toughest and most competitive in the world, does this automatically mean that football in this country — both as a game and in its organisation — is the best in the world? The 1974 World Cup showed that it is not. The quality of much of the play in Germany emphasised that British soccer is now some way behind South American, West German and Dutch football.

It takes a long time to change the way a country plays football. Britain may have the best competitive League in the world, but in the next ten years or so football in this country will not only have to adapt to a new style of play, but it will also have to examine how it spends its money — stadiums need to be rebuilt, spectators need to be more comfortable. Changes will have to made at the top and bottom; directors of clubs must become more adventurous and senior officials at the FA and Football League more aware of the problems that face football in this country. At the other end of the scale, the wastage of young footballers must be halted. Too many potentially good footballers never make the grade. Football in this country is good and the world has learnt a lot from our style. But in return we must learn from other countries not only to re-examine the way we *play* football but how we *run* football.

*Old Trafford, home of Manchester United. An **average** of more than 48,000 people watched United in the 1974/5 season when they were in the **second** Division. Manchester United is one of*

the few rich clubs in the League. (This is the goal that put United back in the First Division–Gerry Daly shoots past Fulham keeper Peter Mellor.)

The future

Apart from selling players, League clubs get most of their money from selling lottery and bingo tickets, something which has nothing to do with football at all. In fact, if clubs relied on the money that spectators paid then most would go out of business very quickly. Even with the money that clubs make from other activities clubs are finding it very hard to survive. What could be done?

1 The Government could give the Football League money each year. This money could *not* be used for buying players.

2 Clubs could combine with their local councils to make their grounds into leisure centres, open to everyone throughout the week.

3 Big firms could sponsor a club—give it their name for publicity purposes and provide money to keep it going.

4 The Football League could allow sponsors to 'buy' each of the Divisions, eg Ford Division I, Rothman's Division II. The money would be shared among the clubs in each division.

Some famous football clubs are now so poor that they might soon have to drop out of the League. New steps are needed quickly to protect the future of League football.

16
YOUR CLUB DOSSIER

There are ninety-two clubs in the Football League. They all play football differently; they are all run differently. Each club has its own ideas on the best way to score goals, the best strip to wear, how to look after the players, how to organise travelling. Different groundsmen have different methods of keeping the pitch in shape; managers have their own methods of keeping the club in order.

So, as well as supporting your team to the championship, why not prepare a special dossier on them? A special report on the other side of football. Get a scrapbook and divide it into sections, rather like this book — boots, strip, referees, pitch, goals, nets, trainers and so on. For every match you see try and build up a picture of *everything* to do with your club. For a particular game your dossier might read something like this:

BOOTS Five players wore Adidas, two Gola, two Stylo, two unidentified. The ground was hard so moulded soles were worn. Smith seemed to have a brand new pair of boots. Evans changed his boots at half-time.

STRIP Long-sleeve 'V' neck. Usual colour. Jones, however, had short-sleeve shirt in second half. Lace-up shorts used for first time. New type of number on shirt. All but two players wore shin-pads.

OFFICIALS Old type of strip worn by ref. Linesmen in new shirts. Ref consulted linesman three times during game.

BALL 32-panel Mitre. White.

NETS Orange, close weave.

PITCH Very hard. Grass cut in circular fashion from centre.

POLICE About fifty. Twenty-four St John's Ambulance men.

TRAINER Came on twice. Used PR spray and sponge. Carried red bag, unmarked.

SUB In tracksuit. Did not come on.

Dave Thomas about to congratulate David Johnson after scoring for England against Wales in May 1975. What else can you spot in the picture? Dave Thomas is wearing Gola boots, Johnson Puma. Both players are wearing England strip made by Admiral. Note lace-up shorts with cutaway speed vent, short-sleeved summer shirts and the pattern made by the cellular nylon on the shirts. The nets are the old type, the posts elliptical.

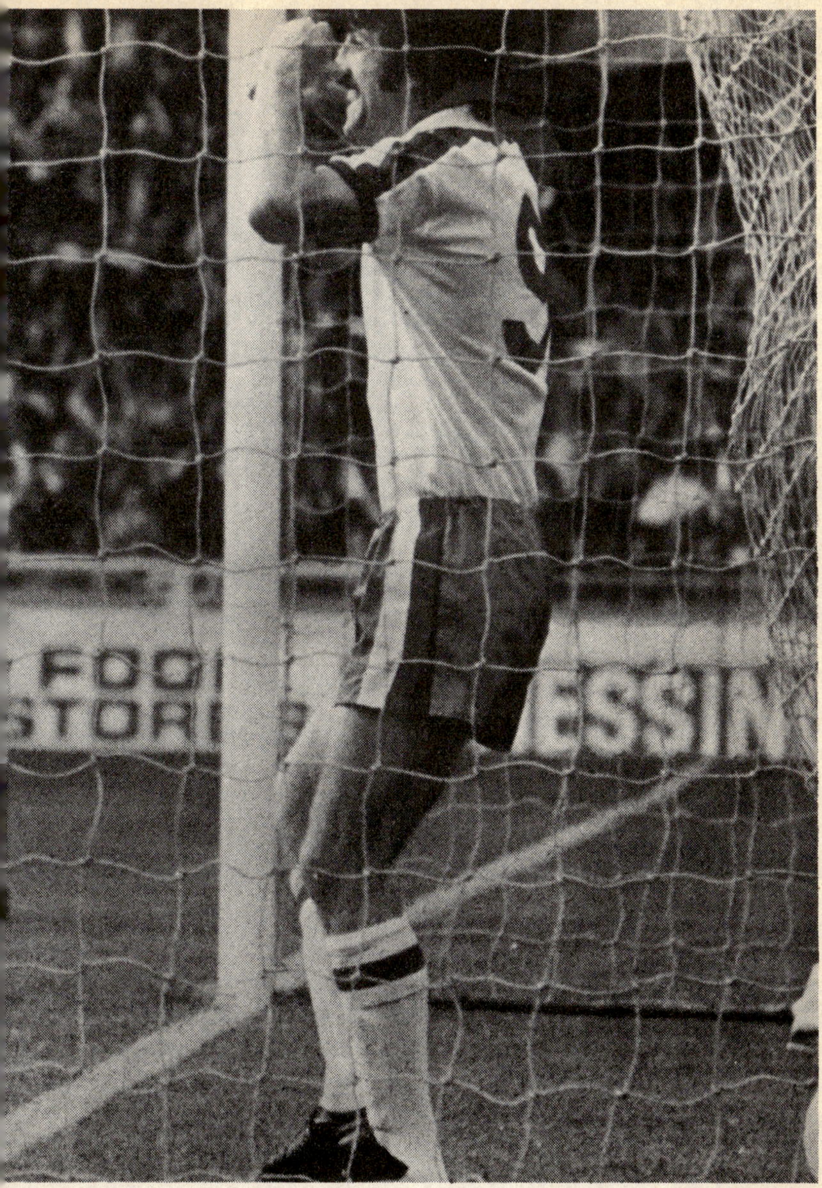
FOO
STORE
ESSIN

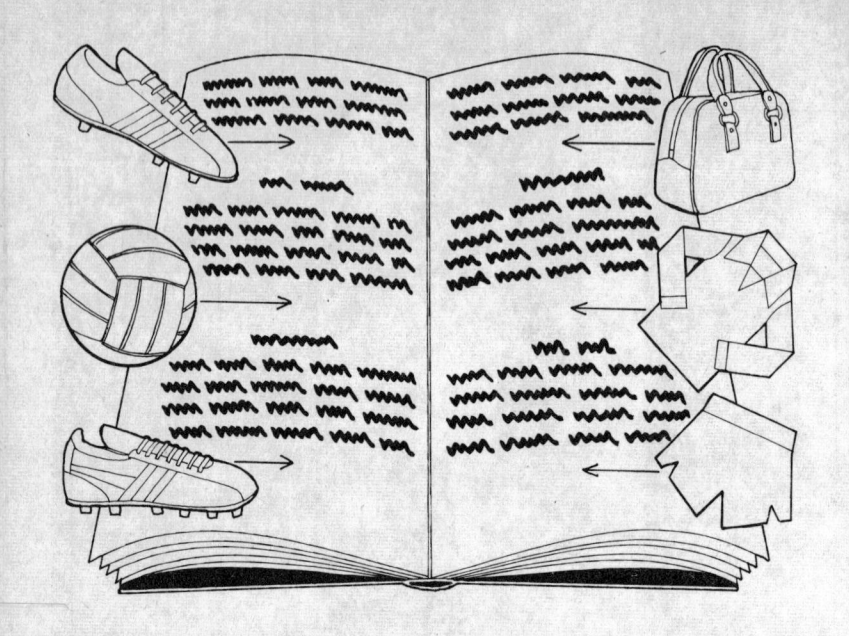

A club dossier.

For every match you see make a list like this; as the season goes by you will gradually build up a picture of your team and club. You will notice that certain things change from game to game, and when visiting an away side you will spot ways in which that club does things differently. During the course of a season you will notice changes that perhaps you would not have spotted before. Slowly you will find that you have written a valuable and unusual record of your club, packed with the sort of information you won't find anywhere else.

The big thing about football is that it is always changing — new methods of play, new kit, new ideas. Keep track of the changes and watch football develop. In just five years time you will be surprised just how much has happened.

Your dossier will become another *Football: how much do you really know?*

WORDS

CLEATS
Wedge-shaped grips, usually on the sole of a training shoe.
FA
The Football Association. All football clubs in this country—large or small—belong to the FA. The Football League controls the clubs in the Football League.
FIFA
Fédération Internationale de Football Association. The international body controlling football throughout the world.
GATE
The number of people attending a match.
MOULDED-SOLE
The studs and sole of a football shoe made in one piece, usually of rubber or plastic.
PANELS
Footballs are made up with panels—leather or plastic. Professional balls are made with 18 or 32 panels.
PITCH
The dictionary definition of 'pitch' is to 'make fast, to settle, to keep in place'. So the area of grass where a team plays is a pitch because it is there permanently.
PFA
Professional Footballers' Association. The union to which all professional footballers belong. It helps sort out problems over contracts, discipline, transfers etc.
SOCCER
The word comes from 'As*soc*iation' Football.
STADIUM
A large arena with splendid facilities.
STRIP
Kit. The word comes from the fact that footballers have to 'strip off' their clothes before putting on their kit.
TIE-UPS
Used by players to keep their socks up. Usually strips of cloth, although teams like Leeds United have special tie-ups which show each player's number.

UPPERS
The top part of a football shoe. Usually the uppers wear out long before the soles.

BOOKS ON FOOTBALL

The Football League Handbook   Available from The Football League, Lytham St Annes, Lancashire FY8 1JG

The Football Association Handbook   Available from the FA, 16, Lancaster Gate, London W2 3LW

Both these books are packed with interesting facts hidden among the 'official' language.

Rothman's Football Yearbook   The best book of soccer facts and figures

ACKNOWLEDGEMENTS

The author would like to thank everyone who helped in the preparation of this book, particularly Arsenal, Darlington, Oxford and Aston Villa Football Clubs, Gola, Stylo, Admiral and Adidas, and Bob Baldwin of the Football League.

PHOTOGRAPHIC ACKNOWLEDGEMENTS

The publishers would like to thank the following for permission to reproduce the photographs in this book:

Press Association, pages 20, 21 (top), 30, 36, 89, 118-119; Andrew Whittuck, pages 10, 11, 52, 53, 54, 55, 57, 62, 66, 68, 69, 77, 84-85, 86, 95, 97, 99, 101; Associated Press, pages 73, 113; Keystone, pages 21 (bottom), 37; Fox Photos, page 31; London Weekend Television, page 106; Mary Evans Picture Library, page 109; *Oxford Mail,* page 83.

INDEX

action replay, 102, 103
Aldershot F.C., 14
apprentice, 76
Arsenal F.C., 8-12, 14, 22, 24, 27, 29, 30, 34, 36, 38, 51, 53, 54, 56, 58, 60, 63, 70, 71, 75, 80, 82, 83, 87, 92, 96, 100, 102, 116
assessors, 45
Aston Villa F.C., 7, 52, 68, 69, 86, 95, 96, 97, 98, 101
ball, Stuart Surridge 'Cobbler', 18
Bateman, Les, 55
BBC, 104, 105
Bell, Colin, 37
Best, George, 116
Blackpool F.C., 30, 104
Bolton Wanderers F.C., 104
'book', the, 46
Bristol City F.C., 116
Brodie, J. A., 62
Burnley F.C., 80
Burtenshaw, Norman, 50
Cardiff F.C., 63
card, red, 46
card, yellow, 46
centre spot, 14
Charlton Athletic F.C., 116
Charlton, Bobby, 74
Chelsea F.C., 101, 116
Chivers, Martin, 38
Clarke, Colin, 83
Clough, Brian, 80, 90
corner, a, 16
corner flags, 16
Coventry City F.C., 88, 116
crash barriers, 98
crossbar, the, 60
crown, the, 54
Cruyff, Johann, 112, 113, 116
Daly, Gerry, 119
Darlington F.C., 8-12, 14, 22, 29, 34, 58, 60, 70, 80, 82, 83, 87, 92, 102
Doncaster Rovers F.C., 13, 14
Dougan, Derek, 90
drainage, 54
East Germany, 60
England, 37, 39, 104
Everton F.C., 82, 116

Football Association, The, 81
F.A. Cup Final, 22, 45
Football League, The, 111
footballer, professional, 82
Fulham F.C., 14
goalkeeper, 39
goalposts, the, 60, 61
goals, 60-64
groundsman, 51-59
Halifax F.C., 14
Hall, Brian, 90
Heighway, Steve, 90
Hereford F.C., 14
hooliganism, 100
Huddersfield F.C., 63
ITV, 104, 105
James, Alex, 30
James, Leighton, 13
Johnson, David, 122, 123
Keegan, Kevin, 74
Kirkpatrick, Roger, 47, 48
kit, 32-42
Law, J. J., 29
League Merit List, the, 45
Leeds United F.C., 32, 36, 38, 63
Leicester City F.C., 38, 58
lines, 16
linesmen, 43-50
Liverpool F.C., 27, 82, 88, 90, 108
Manchester City F.C., 13, 34, 56, 63
Manchester United F.C., 14, 63, 101, 108, 118, 119
Matthews, Stanley, 31
Mellor, Peter, 119
Middlesbrough F.C., 63
nets, the, 62-63
Newcastle United F.C., 63, 67, 100
Northampton F.C., 14
Nottingham Forest F.C., 41, 63
numbers, 38-39
Oldham F.C., 14
Orient F.C., 13, 14
Osgood, Peter, 38
Oxford United F.C., 55, 73, 78, 79, 83, 85
penalty spot, 14
pitch, the, 13-16
player, amateur, 75

police, 98
Portsmouth F.C., 67
posts, 16
   flag, 16
Q.P.R. F.C., 32
Referee Coaching Officer, 50
referees, 43-50
Revie, Don, 32
rules, the, 108-111
St. John's Ambulance, 11, 98, 100
schoolboy player, 75
   associate, 76
   professional, 76
secretary, the, 11
Shankly, Bill, 27
Shilton, Peter, 39, 40
shin-pads, 30-42
shirts, 30-42
socks, 30-42
Southampton F.C., 14
spectators, 98-101
Spurs F.C., 12, 67
Stoke City F.C., 39, 40
studs, 27
Summers, Gerry, 73
Sunderland F.C., 67
television, 90
Thomas, Dave, 122
throw-in, a, 16
trainer, 92-95
training, 83-88
travelling, 88
Vogts, Berne, 37
Wembley, 14, 19, 70
West Germany, 37
West Ham F.C., 13, 14, 63
Widdowson, Sam, 41
Wolverhampton Wanderers F.C., 72
World Cup 1953, 104; 1966, 19;
   1970, 104; 1974, 117
Wrexham F.C., 14